BADGES AND INSIGNIA OF THE
ELITE FORCES

BADGES AND INSIGNIA OF THE
ELITE FORCES

LEROY THOMPSON

◄ During an award
ceremony both Airborne
Command and XVIII
Airborne Corps shoulder
sleeve insignia are in wear.

ARMS AND
ARMOUR

Arms and Armour
An imprint of the Cassell Group
Wellington House, 125 Strand
London WC2R 0BB
www.cassell.co.uk

British Library Cataloguing in Publication Data
A catalogue record for this book is available from the British Library
ISBN 1-85409-511-0

Colour plates by Malcolm McGregor

Distributed in the USA by
Sterling Publishing Co. Inc.
387 Park Avenue South
New York, NY 10016-8810

Printed in Hong Kong by Wing King Tong Co. Ltd.

CONTENTS

ACKNOWLEDGEMENTS

Many people have given me assistance in preparing this book, but a few should be singled out for special thanks. I should first like to thank Harry Pugh, to whom most of us who are interested in élite unit insignia owe a salute for acting as the pathfinder in the subject. Others include Ken and Pam Lewis, Hal Feldman, Lou DiPonziano, Joe Gervasi, Adrian Bohlen, Rene Smeets, Pete McDermott, and all the other members of Chute and Dagger.

▼In 1961 this member of the Special Forces now wears the Special Forces arrowhead shoulder sleeve insignia but still wears the parachute badge and oval as a beret badge. (US Army)

INTRODUCTION

In defining the term 'élite military units' one always finds certain confusion. In Great Britain, for example, many would class any of the Guards Regiments as élite, while in France, the Meharistes who galloped across the Sahara on their camels are considered élite. For purposes of this book, however, I have considered as élite those units that are parachute-qualified, or that have been trained as Commandos, Rangers or long-range patrollers. In some cases I have also included anti-terrorist units which, when military, definitely fall within these parameters and when police probably do.

Although as originally conceived this work would have covered such élite units from their genesis during the Second World War until the present, the fact that Second World War insignia have already been covered in some detail elsewhere and the necessity to limit space have caused me to start in the post-war period and end at about the Falklands War. Due to the availability of the excellent works on parachute badges by Bragg and Turner, I have also not included parachute badges (or brevets) but have instead concentrated on beret badges or flashes, shoulder sleeve insignia, pocket patches, collar insignia, distinctive insignia, and other types of qualification badges.

It would be naïve on my part to claim completeness for this work since many insignia worn by élite units are produced in extremely limited numbers and in great variety. It probably would have been possible, in fact, to write an entire book on US insignia alone, and certainly it would be possible to do just that for French insignia. But having had to be selective, I have sought to choose those most likely to be encountered or those of particular interest.

Leroy Thompson
St. Louis, Missouri

▶ Two US Congressional Medal of Honor winners – Colonel Lewis Millett and FSG Garry Littrell – wearing both US parachute brevets and Vietnamese Ranger qualification badges; note that Littrell also wears Air Assault brevet and Millett wears a French para brevet. (Society of Vietnamese Ranger)

AFRICA

RHODESIA

Rhodesia's initial parachute-qualified unit was the squadron which volunteered for service with the British SAS in Malaya. Later designated C Squadron, this unit was disbanded upon its return to Rhodesia, but was reformed in 1962 and continued to serve on special operations within Rhodesia and across her borders until that country ceased to exist. To some extent an offshoot of the SAS, the Tracker Combat Unit and other formations, were the Selous Scouts, a highly trained unit specializing in pseudo counter-insurgency operations as well as cross-border raids. The Rhodesian

Light Infantry should also be mentioned since as counter-insurgency progressed this unit received parachute training as well. Many of its 'Fire Forces' were parachuted in as blocking forces to cut off guerrillas fleeing the country. Often jumping from extremely low altitude, members of the RLI more than once made as many as three combat jumps in one day thus surpassing even the French paras in Indo-China in the number of combat jumps.

Rhodesian SAS troops wore the same sand-coloured beret as the British SAS; Sealous Scouts wore a brown beret, and the RLI a green beret.

PLATE 1: RHODESIA

1 SAS cap badge
2 SAS collar insignia
3 Selous Scouts LTC shoulder slide
4 Selous Scouts shoulder slide (major's rank)
5 Selous Scouts shoulder slide (captain)
6 Selous Scouts shoulder slide (lieutenant)
7 Light Infantry beret badge
8 Selous Scouts beret badge
9 Selous Scouts stable belt

▶ Selous Scouts captain, clean shaven which was not the norm in the Scouts, shows the beret badge on the chocolate-brown beret and the shoulder slides with rank and unit ID. (David Scott-Donelan)

SOUTH AFRICA

The first South African parachute unit was the 2nd Mobile Watch, which was converted to the 1st Parachute Battalion in April 1961. This unit saw action

against insurgents in South West Africa in 1966. Initially, trained reservists served with 1st Parachute Battalion as well, but in 1971, 2nd Parachute Battalion was formed as a Citizen Force (Reserve) unit. Members of 2nd Parachute Battalion saw action during Opera-

PLATE 1 CONTINUED: SOUTH AFRICA

1 Original cloth 1st Parachute Battalion shoulder insignia
2 Variant of No. 1
3 Early 1st Parachute Battalion insignia
4 1st Parachute Battalion shoulder arc

5 Afrikaans version of No. 4
6 Enamelled metal 1st Parachute Battalion shoulder crest
7 Cloth version of No. 6
8 1st Parachute Battalion pocket crest
9 1st Parachute Battalion arm flash on hanger
10 44th Parachute Brigade arm flash

PLATE 1

1

2

7

8

SELOUS SCOUTS — SELOUS SCOUTS — SELOUS SCOUTS — SELOUS SCOUTS

3   4   5   6

9

1

2

3

1 PARA BN

4

1 VALSK BN

5

6

7

8

9

10

tion 'Savanna' in the Angolan Civil War. In 1977 3rd Parachute Battalion was established as another reserve formation. Companies from all three battalions saw extensive action in South West Africa on COIN ops.

In April 1978, 44 Parachute Brigade was formed; 320 members of the airborne forces taking part in a jump on a SWAPO base deep in Angola only about a month later in Operation 'Reindeer'.

Currently, parachutists must qualify by undergoing four weeks of airborne training which includes eleven jumps. To become free-fall-qualified requires a 3-weeks' free-fall course including about fifty free-fall jumps. Fifty jumps are also required to be awarded the advanced parachutist rank. Advanced parachutists may undergo instructor training.

There are also South African Police task force members who are parachute-qualified. Of particular interest were the Rail and Harbour Police Task Force which had a counter-terrorist role. Their qualification course included SWAT, explosives and weapons training, and fifteen jumps including five free-fall.

Special forces duties within the South African armed forces are handled by the Reconnaissance Commandos, each of which had specialized duties. Fourth Reconnaissance Commando, for example, has the amphibious/combat swimmer mission while 5th Recce Commando, formed initially from former Rhodesian Selous Scouts, has the pseudo operations mission.

Not strictly part of the South African élite forces but related are those airborne/special forces of the Black homelands within South Africa. Bophuthatswana has a special forces unit located at Lehurutshe Military Base near the Botswana border. Of company strength, this unit has a counter-insurgency and counter-terrorism mission. In addition to their parachute wings, airborne-qualified members of the Special Forces company wear burgundy-coloured berets. Ciskei initially trained a small special forces unit of their police, but in 1982 this unit was expanded to 'squadron' strength. Transkei has a Special Forces Regiment which was initially trained by Ron Reid Daly, former commander of the Selous Scouts. Based at Port St. Johns, the Transkei Special Forces wear a maroon beret. At the time of writing, Transkei is also considering converting their 1st Infantry Battalion to an airborne battalion.

PLATE 2: SOUTH AFRICA AND SOUTH AFRICAN HOMELANDS

11 2nd Parachute Battalion
12 3rd Parachute Battalion
13 4th Parachute Battalion
14 18th Light Artillery Regiment
15 44th AA Regiment
16 44th Maintenance Unit
17 44th Field Workshop
18 44th Field Engineers
19 44th Signal Unit
20 Subdued cloth arm flash for 2nd Parachute Battalion; such subdued flashes have also been used for the 3rd and 4th Prachute Battalions and the 18th Light Artillery Regiment
21 Ciskei Special Forces arm flash

Note Nos. 22–25 are fake items which were never adopted and are included for information
22 Proposed 2nd Reconnaissance Commando insignia in metal

23 Proposed 2nd Reconnaissance Commando insignia in cloth
24 Variant of No 22 in metal
25 Proposed 1st Reconnaissance Commando insignia in cloth
26 HQ Special Forces arm flash
27 1st Reconnaissance Commando arm flash
28 2nd Reconnaissance Commando arm flash
29 4th Reconnaissance Commando arm flash
30 5th Reconnaissance Commando arm flash; the presence of the Selous Scouts parachute wings on the badge
31 Early 5th Reconnaissance track suit patch
32 Ciskei special forces beret badge
33 Ciskei special forces collar insignia
34 Transkei special forces beret badge
35 Transkei special forces/airborne arm flash

PLATE 2

11

12

13

14

15

16

17

18

19

20

21

22

23

24

25

26

27

28

29

30

31

32

33

34

35

PLATE 3: CONGO

The later history of Parachute/Commando forces in the former Belgian Congo are related below under Zaire. Of particular interest from the time when it was the Congo are the various 'Commando' units formed of white mercenaries or of blacks trained by white mercenaries during the 1960s.

1 Commando beret badge
2 Commando beret badge, worn by Mike Hoare's 5 Commando among others
3 Commando beret badge
4–10 Various shoulder/pocket insignia worn by Commando units in the Congo; note the presence of the sword and star in most.

▼Congolese 'Airborne Commandos' show a diversity of uniform and equipment.

PLATE 3 CONTINUED: ZAIRE

While Zaire was still the Congo, white mercenaries trained a Commando Battalion which acted as a presidential guard unit. Later US Special Forces personnel trained parachute personnel as did the Israelis. By 1967, members of the parachute battalions were used against white mercenaries. By the mid-1970s there were at least a half-dozen parachute battalions as well as Commando battalions. In April 1977 and May 1978, members of Zaire's Parachute Regiment made combat jumps against Katangan rebels. Generally, Zaire's paras are rated among the best in black Africa.

1 Parachutist Commando beret badge
2 Commando beret badge
3 Commando instructor brevet
4 Commando A Brevet
5 Commando B Brevet
6 Guerrilla Warfare brevet
7 Guerrilla Warfare instructor

PLATE 3

1

2

3

4

5

6

7

8

9

10

1

2

3

4

5

6

7

THE AMERICAS

UNITED STATES OF AMERICA

All four branches of the US armed forces contain units which can be termed 'élite'. Within the Army are the Airborne, Air Assault, Rangers, and Special Forces including the Delta anti-terrorist unit; within the Navy are the SEAL (Sea, Air, Land) Teams; within the Marine Corps the Recons and the ANGLICOs, and within the Air Force the PJs (Pararescuemen), the CCTs (Combat Control Teams), and the men of the Combat Weather units. In many cases training for these various units overlaps, with a substantial amount of cross-training between the units taking place. Virtually all share basic airborne qualification

PLATE 4: US BERET FLASHES

1 US Army John F. Kennedy Center for Military Assistance

2 Special Forces School: Originally these were made by the instructors or their wives who took white felt and cut it to shape; for a period during the 1960s a version in naugahide was also worn; today, however, a machine-made version is worn

3 1st Special Forces Group (Airborne)

4 1st Special Forces Group (Airborne) incorporating the black 'mourning band' added after the death of President Kennedy, the patron of the Special Forces. This flash may be found with both ⅛in and ¹/₁₆in wide mourning bands

5 3rd Special Forces Group (Airborne)

6 5th Special Forces Group (Airborne): the original 5th Group flash and reinstated for use by the Group a few years ago

7 5th Special Forces Group (Airborne): the flash adopted after the deployment of the 5th to Vietnam and incorporating the colours of that country's flag; this version continued to be worn by the 5th throughout the 1970s and on into the 1980s

8 5th Special Forces Group (Airborne): flash locally made in Vietnam and incorporating the skull and crossbones of the 'Bright Light Teams'

9 5th Special Forces Group (Airborne): flash locally made in Vietnam and incorporating officers' or warrant officers' rank insignia, most often found with captain's or 1st lieutenant's rank

10 5th Special Forces Group (Airborne): flash locally made in Vietnam and incorporating the Special Forces DI, which was worn on the beret flash by enlisted personnel

11 6th Special Forces Group (Airborne)

12 7th Special Forces Group (Airborne)

13 8th Special Forces Group (Airborne)

14 10th Special Forces Group (Airborne)

15 11th Special Forces Group (Airborne)

16 12th Special Forces Group (Airborne)

17 Reserve Components Special Forces: this flash was originally worn by all US Army Reserve and National Guard Special Forces Groups

18 19th Special Forces Group (Airborne)

19 20th Special Forces Group (Airborne): original flash worn by this National Guard Special Forces Group

20 20th Special Forces Group (Airborne): current version of this group's flash

21 Special Forces Detachment Europe: note that this flash incorporates the colours of the Federal Republic of Germany's flag

22 46th Special Forces Company (Airborne): this flash for the Special Forces personnel in Thailand during the Vietnam War period incorporates the colours of the Thai flag

23 Special Forces Detachment Korea: this flash, still in wear by Special Forces personnel assigned to Korea, incorporates the colours of the ROK flag

24 US Army John F. Kennedy–Walter Reed Army Institute of Research Field Epidemilogical Survey Team (Airborne). Popularly known as the FEST flash, this very rare flash was worn by Special Forces medical personnel sent to South-east Asia to survey diseases likely to be encountered by US military personnel serving there

25 USARVITG-FANK: this flash was worn by those Special Forces personnel involved in training Cambodian troops

26 22nd Special Warfare Aviation Company

27 Ranger flash worn in Vietnam

28 Variation of the Ranger flash in Vietnam

29 Another variation of the Ranger flash in Vietnam

30 LRRP (Long-Range Reconnaissance Patrol) flash worn in Vietnam by members of the 1/4 or 3/4 Cavalry

PLATE 4

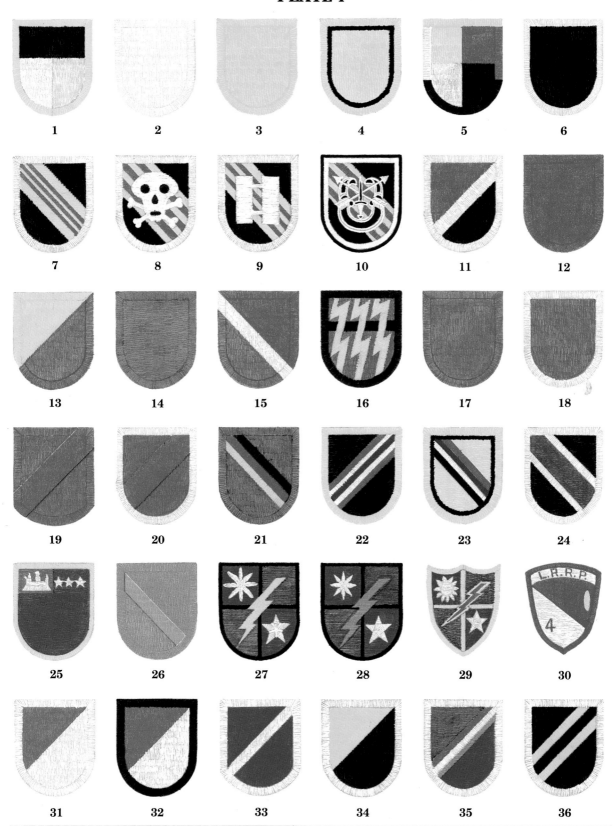

1

2

3

4

5

6

7

8

9

10

11

12

13

14

15

16

17

18

19

20

21

22

23

24

25

26

27

28

29

30

31

32

33

34

35

36

achieved through attending the 3-weeks' basic parachute course at Fort Benning, Georgia. The Ranger course lasts 58 days and by pushing the trainees through twenty or more hours of training per day, compacts about six months' training into one-third that time. The Special Forces Q-Course (Qualification Course) lasts seventeen weeks (more for combat medics) above basic airborne qualification. The Air Assault course lasts two weeks but it is an intensive two weeks. BUD/S (Basic Underwater Demolition/ SEAL) training lasts six months, while in the Marine Corps Basic Amphibious Recon School lasts seven weeks. Within the Air Forces, PJ training lasts up to eleven months in a course that includes parachute, scuba, survival, medical and various other types of training. CCT and Combat Weather are somewhat similar though the specialized training in air traffic control and meteorology are substituted for that in combat medicine.

Traditionally, there have been three distinctions which help identify most members of US élite units – the beret, trousers bloused into jump boots, and special insignia, especially parachutist's wings. First to wear the beret were the Special Forces, still known to many as the 'Green Berets', in fact, based on their headgear. Special Forces has remained the only unit to wear the green beret. Airborne troops, CCTs, and PJs all currently wear the maroon beret, though the CCTs previously wore a dark-blue one. The Air Force Combat Security Police (a Ranger-trained élite light infantry unit of the Vietnam War) also wore blue berets as have the 101st Airborne (Air Assault), and the Combat

31 Flash worn by some airborne elements of the 17th Armored Cavalry in Vietnam (probably the cavalry elements assigned to the 82nd or 101st Airborne Divisions or the 173rd Airborne Brigade)

32 A variation of the 17th Cavalry flash

33 Company D (Ranger) 151st Infantry (Indiana National Guard)

34 Original Ranger flash of 1st Battalion (Ranger) 75th Infantry, which continued to be worn by Ranger depot instructors after the adoption of the second-pattern flash below

35 Second Pattern Ranger flash worn by 1st and 2nd Battalions (Ranger) 75th Infantry until replaced after the formation of the 3rd Ranger Battalion

36 Company F (Ranger) 425th Infantry (Michigan Army National Guard)

PLATE 5: U.S. BERET FLASHES CONTINUED

37 Flash of 28th Infantry Detachment (Pathfinder), 28th Aviation Battalion (Indiana National Guard); note that this flash was initially formed by cutting in half subdued and colour versions of the 28th Division's shoulder sleeve insignia and sewing one-half of each together

38 Company C (Airborne), 4th Battalion, 9th Infantry, 172nd Infantry Brigade (Alaska)

39 Company C (Airborne), 4th Battalion, 23rd Infantry, 172nd Infantry Brigade (Alaska)

40 Company C (Airborne), 1st Battalion, 60th Infantry, 172nd Infantry Brigade (Alaska)

41 HHC, 71st Airborne Brigade (separate), (Texas Army National Guard); now obsolete

42 1st Battalion (Airborne), 143rd Infantry, 71st Airborne Brigade (separate) (Texas Army National Guard); now obsolete

43 2nd Battalion (Airborne), 143rd Infantry, 71st Airborne Brigade (separate) (Texas Army National Guard); now obsolete

44 HQ, 82nd Airborne Division

45 1st Brigade (Airborne), 82nd Airborne Division

46 2nd Brigade (Airborne), 82nd Airborne Division

47 3rd Brigade (Airborne), 82nd Airborne Division

48 1st Battalion (Airborne), 325th Infantry

49 2nd Battalion (Airborne), 325th Infantry

50 3rd Battalion (Airborne), 325th Infantry

51 Company E (Anti-Armor), 325th Infantry

52 1st Battalion (Airborne), 504th Infantry

53 2nd Battalion (Airborne), 504th Infantry

54 Company E (Anti-Armor), 504th Infantry

55 1st Battalion (Airborne), 505th Infantry

56 2nd Battalion (Airborne), 505th Infantry –

57 1st Battalion (Airborne), 508th Infantry

58 2nd Battalion (Airborne), 508th Infantry

59 82nd Airborne Division Artillery

60 3rd Battalion (Vulcan) (Airborne), 4th Air Defense Artillery

61 82nd Airborne Division DISCOM

62 407th S&S Battalion

63 307th Medical Battalion

64 307th Engineer Battalion

65 618th Engineer Company (L.E.M.)

66 82nd Signal Battalion; note this flash was made in error with the pentagon upside down (see 67)

67 82nd Signal Battalion

68 82nd Aviation Battalion

69 1st Squadron, 17th Cavalry

70 4th Battalion (Airborne) (Light), 68th Armor; note all flashes from nos 44 to 70 are for 82nd Airborne Division units, though some are now obsolete

71 HQ, XVIII Airborne Corps

72 XVIII Airborne Corps Artillery

PLATE 5

37　38　39　40　41　42

43　44　45　46　47　48

49　50　51　52　53　54

55　56　57　58　59　60

61　62　63　64　65　66

67　68　69　70　71　72

Weather troops who wore a blue/grey beret. The Rangers wear a black beret, while the SEALs have at times worn both black and camouflage berets though neither was official.

'Official' is an operant word when discussing US élite insignia, too, as only a limited amount of the insignia associated with US élite forces was ever authorized. Many, but certainly not all, beret flashes usually worn behind a unit crest of DI (Distinctive Insignia) were authorized; most DIs were authorized; only the major unit SSIs (Shoulder Sleeve Insignia) were normally authorized, and few pocket patches have ever been authorized. The Vietnam War especially saw a profusion of fascinating pocket patches made by local small tailor shops and worn on casual clothing, inside berets, or on the pockets of utility clothing. Because these locally made pocket patches are so fascinating and so rare they have now been widely faked, and one must be very careful in adding them to a collection as the prices now asked are frequently quite high.

◄ Member of the 82nd Airborne Division applies camouflage paint; note the subdued version of the 82nd shoulder sleeve insignia. (US Army)

PLATE 6: U.S. BERET FLASHES CONTINUED

73 50th Signal Battalion (XVIII Airborne Corps)
74 20th Engineering Brigade (XVIII Airborne Corps)
75 20th Engineer Battalion, 101st Airborne Division
76 27th Engineer Battalion (Combat) (Airborne)
77 600th Quartermaster Company (AER)
78 612th Quartermaster Company (AD)
79 313th CWIE Battalion
80 ACE Board, Army Material Command
81 US Army Airborne Board
82 503rd MP Battalion, 16th MP Brigade
83 HQ, 101st Airborne Division
84 1st Brigade, 101st Airborne Division
85 2nd Brigade, 101st Airborne Division
86 3rd Brigade, 101st Airborne Division
87 3rd Battalion, 187th Infantry
88 1st Battalion, 327th Infantry
89 2nd Battalion, 327th Infantry
90 1st Battalion, 501st Infantry
91 1st Battalion, 502nd Infantry

92 2nd Battalion, 502nd Infantry
93 1st Battalion, 503rd Infantry
94 2nd Battalion, 503rd Infantry
95 1st Battalion, 506th Infantry
96 101st Airborne Division Artillery; note that the 7th Special Forces Group (Airborne) and the 82nd Airborne Division Artillery wear this same flash
97 1st Battalion (Vulcan), 3rd ADA
98 101st Airborne DISCOM (Division Support Command)
99 101st MP Company
100 326th Engineer Battalion
101 501st Signal Battalion
102 2nd Squadron, 17th Cavalry
103 101st Aviation Group
104 US Army Forces Command (FORSCOM)
105 29th Transportation Battalion
106 86th Combat Support Hospital
107 5th Infantry Platoon (Pathfinder) (Airborne) (97th ARCOM)
108 Company E (Ranger), 65th Infantry (Puerto Rico Army National Guard); obsolete

PLATE 6

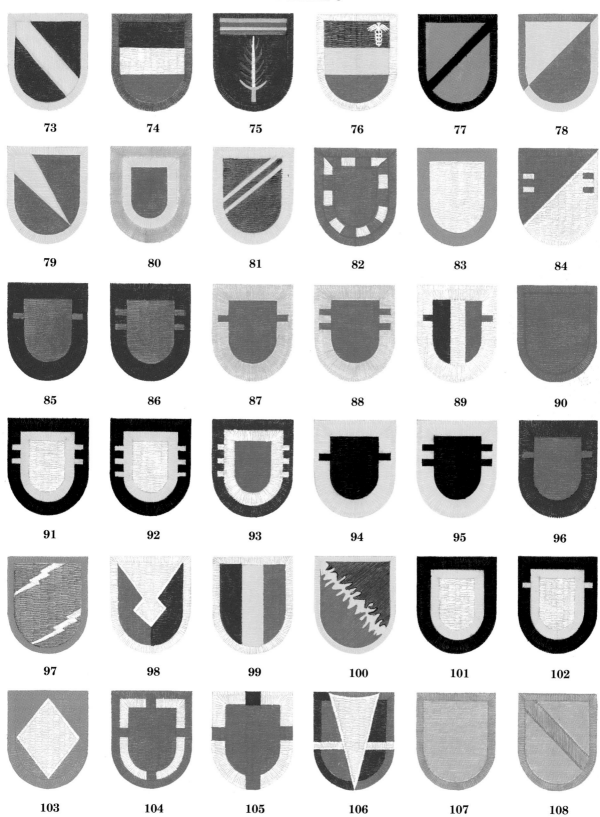

73 74 75 76 77 78

79 80 81 82 83 84

85 86 87 88 89 90

91 92 93 94 95 96

97 98 99 100 101 102

103 104 105 106 107 108

PLATE 7: BERET FLASHES AND SPECIAL FORCES DISTINCTIVE INSIGNIA

109 Flash worn by advisers from the 1st SFG (Airborne) from 1961 to 1963; originally of quilted material

110 Flash reportedly worn by Special Forces personnel working with the CIA in Laos in the early 1960s; made from camouflaged parachute silk

111 Parachute oval for 1st Special Operations Command (Airborne); note that almost all of the beret flashes illustrated would have a matching parachute oval to be worn behind the parachute wings to designate unit assignment. The Special Forces Groups also at one time had what were known as 'striker bars', a bar bearing the same colours/pattern as the flash and worn on the beret by those personnel who might be assigned to a Group who were not fully Special Forces qualified

112 Flash for 1st SOCOM (Airborne)

113 Flash for Joint Special Operations Command

114 Flash for the LRRP Platoon, 11th Armored Cavalry Regiment in Vietnam; this flash exists in both locally hand-made and machine-made forms

115 Flash for Company E (LRP), 50th Infantry (9th Infantry Division) in Vietnam; this flash exists with variations in both hand- and machine-made forms

116 Flash for 74th Infantry Detachment (LRP), 173rd Airborne Brigade in Vietnam

117 Flash for Company A (Airborne), 3rd Battalion, 5th Infantry (193rd Infantry Brigade)

118 Flash worn by HQ personnel for the Puerto Rico National Guard and also reportedly by Company E (Ranger), 65th Infantry

119 Flash for the US Army Parachute Team (The Golden Knights)

120 Flash worn by USAF Combat Weather personnel

121 Flash for the 1/143rd Infantry

122 Flash for Company C (Pathfinder), 509th Infantry (1st Aviation Brigade)

123 Flash for 525th Military Intelligence Brigade (CEWI) (Airborne) (XVIII Airborne Corps)

124 Flash for 561st Maintenance Battalion

1 Distinctive Insignia for the Special Warfare Center and Institute for Military Assistance

2 DI for 1st Psychological Operations Battalion

3 DI for 77th Special Forces Group (Airborne)

4 DI for 1st Special Forces

5 Beret badge worn by the 10th Special Forces Group (Airborne) before the adoption of a beret flash from 1955–62

6 DI for 10th Special Forces Group (Airborne)

7 DI worn by 1st Special Operations Command on right shoulder-strap

8 DI worn by 1st SOCOM on left shoulder-strap and beret

9 DI worn by staff of MACV RECONDO School in Vietnam

◀Members of the 77th SFG (Airborne) during guerrilla warfare training. Note that one of the two soldiers is acting as a local indigenous man. The parachute wings and oval were worn as the beret badge, and the Airborne Command shoulder sleeve insignia is being worn. (US Army)

PLATE 7

109

110

111

112

113

114

115

116

117

118

119

120

121

122

123

124

1

2

3

4

5

6

7

8

9

PLATE 8: US SPECIAL FORCES MACV/SOG INSIGNIA – VIETNAM

1 Locally made shoulder sleeve insignia for the 5th Special Forces Group; note that many of the MACV/SOG insignia illustrated can be found in both hand-sewn and machine-sewn versions and possibly in many variants because many of the insignia were re-made for new arrivals 'in country' or new recon team members

2 US Special Forces Vietnam pocket patch, normally encountered encased in plastic and with a pocket hanger; note that the crossed arrows and dagger with green beret motif is used

3 Another Special Forces pocket patch. Like virtually all the other pocket patches worn in Vietnam, this one was unofficial; many of the patches were worn inside the green beret, in fact, sewn to the lining

4 5th Special Forces blazer patch, roughly duplicating the 5th SFG (Airborne) beret flash in Vietnam, though without the white border

5 Pocket patch for the 5th SFG (Airborne) Command and Control element

6 Pocket patch worn by 5th SFG (Airborne) Liaison personnel; 'Lien Lac' translates as liaison

7 Shoulder tab worn by members of Detachment B-36

8 Shoulder tab worn by members of Detachment B-40; note that 'IV CTZ' stands for IV Corps Tactical Zone

9 Pocket patch for Detachment B-52 which controlled Project Delta

10 Patch for Detachment B-53

11 Another patch for B-53 Special Mission Advisory Group; note that this unit's duties included training and advising the Vietnamese Airborne forces, hence the presence of the ARVN airborne beret on the insignia

12 Patch for Detachment B-56, which worked with Project Sigma; 'Tham Bao' means Intelligence; note also the presence of the Greek letter 'Sigma'

13 Patch for Detachment B-57, which worked with Project Gamma; hence the Greek letter 'Gamma'

14 Patch for Detachment A-303 which controlled a Mobile Guerrilla force

15 Shoulder tab worn by members of Detachment A-304

16 Insignia for Detachment A-405; the LLDB were the Vietnamese Special Forces; 'Vien Tham' meant Long Range Recon Patrol. The tiger was frequently worn on MIKE Force insignia

17 Pocket patch worn by members of the 7th Squadron, 1st Cavalry, which provided the helicopter support for the Detachment A-405 MIKE Force

18 Blazer/pocket patch for C-1 Mobile Strike Force

19 Patch for Project Snake Bite; note the US 'Master Blaster' parachute wings incorporated

20 Pocket insignia worn by graduates of the MACV Recondo School

21 Another version of the MACV RECONDO School Pocket insignia; note that there were various other versions of this patch

22 Military Assistance Command Vietnam/Special Operations Group pocket or blazer patch; note the incorporation of aviation wings and the anchor as well as the Special Forces skull denoting the multi-service nature of MACV/SOG

23 Pocket patch for Forward Operations Base 2 personnel; based at Kontum, this unit launched recon and other special missions

24 A variation of FOB-2 pocket patch: note that the skull and shellburst were standard features of many MACV/SOG insignia

25 Pocket patch for FOB-3, which was located at Khe Sanh

▲Special Forces doctor prepares an injection; note the 5th Special Forces Group flash with major or lieutenant-colonel insignia worn on the green beret. Other ranks would wear the Special Forces distinctive insignia on the beret. (US Army)

PLATE 8

1

2

3

4

5

6

7

8

9

10

11

12

13

14

15

16

17

18

19

20

21

22

23

24

25

◀ US adviser wears MIKE Force insignia together with airborne and Ranger tabs. (US Army)

PLATE 9: MACV/SOG INSIGNIA CONTINUED

26 Patch for FOB-4 located at DaNang

27 Patch for Command and Control North; the Command and Control groups replaced the FOBs; CCN was at DaNang

28 Another version of the CCN insignia

29 Still another CCN variation

30 Task Force 1 Advisory Element Communications Section; Task Force 1 replaced CCN; note the antennae attached to the skull and lighting bolts

31 Task Force 1 Advisory Element Medical Section; note that the traditional crossed daggers are replaced by crossed hypodermic needles

32 Command and Control Central pocket patch; CCC was located at Kontum

33 Variation of CCC

34 Variation of CCC

35 Variation of CCC

36 Special Operations Augmentation (CCC) pocket patch; note that the skull wears a hat rather than a beret; 'Augmentation' units were sometimes used to hide the actual assignment of Special Forces personnel to MACV/SOG operations

37 CCC Recon patch; this patch is often referred to as 'The Hulk' patch because of the creature; note that he is kicking a skull

38 Command and Control South pocket patch; CCS was located at Ban Me Thuot

39 Variation of CCS patch

40 Local National Security Group patch; note the Vietnamese airborne wings on patch

41 Recon Team Adder pocket patch; note that many recon teams were named after snakes

42 RT Alabama patch; many other teams were named after states

43 RT Alabama variant

44 RT Alabama patch; 'We Kill For Peace' was a popular, somewhat ironic, Special Forces motto

45 RT Anaconda patch

46 RT Anaconda variation; note that both identify the team as assigned to CCN

47 Another RT Anaconda variation

48 RT Arizona patch; the incorporation of the dragon probably indicates that the indigenous members of the team were Nungs (ethnic Chinese)

49 RT Arizona shoulder tab

50 RT Arkansas patch

PLATE 9

26

27

28

29

30

31

32

33

34

35

36

37

38

39

40

41

42

43

44

45

46

47

48

49

50

PLATE 10: MACV/SOG INSIGNIA CONTINUED

51 RT Arkansas variant; 'Loi Long' means 'Lightning Dragon' as do the Chinese characters; once again this team probably included Nung 'indigs'
52 RT Asp patch
53 RT Asp variation
54 RT California patch
55 RT California variation
56 RT California shoulder tab
57 RT Cobra patch
58 RT Colorado patch
59 RT Colorado variant
60 RT Connecticut patch; 'Epul Ede Ga' means 'Montagnard'
61 RT Crusader patch
62 RT Delaware patch
63 RT Diamondback patch; note that FOB-4 whence the team was launched is included on the insignia
64 RT Florida patch; many of the recon team insignia featured wry humour, in this case the alligator, typical of Florida, is chewing on a VC
65 RT Fork patch
66 RT Georgia patch; note inclusion of Confederate flag and succinct summary of the team's view of Communism
67 RT Hawaii patch; reportedly this was the first RT to have a pocket patch thus helping to start the trend
68 RT Hotcake patch; playing on the team's name, the skull wears a chef's hat rather than the usual beret
69 RT Hunter patch; note that the snake curls around the skull in such a way as to resemble a beret
70 RT Idaho patch
71 RT Illinois patch
72 RT Indiana patch; the Montagnard crossbow in the upper right-hand portion of the shield is indicative of the 'indigs' on the team
73 RT Intruder patch; note the bends carrying the colours of the Republic of Vietnam
74 RT Iowa patch; the Chinese characters mean 'Lightning Tiger'
75 RT Kansas patch
76 RT Kentucky patch; the chess piece is an interesting inclusion representing Kentucky's famed horsebreeding, but also relating to war; in the author's experience some of the hand-made versions of this patch are so well-executed that they almost appear to be machine-made

◄ Members of the 1st Battalion, 75th Rangers at Fort Lewis, WA, apply camo makeup. Note the Ranger scroll. (US Army)

PLATE 10

51

52

53

54

55

56

57

58

59

60

61

62

63

64

65

66

67

68

69

70

71

72

73

74

75

76

PLATE 11: MACV/SOG INSIGNIA CONTINUED

77 RT Kentucky variant

78 RT Krait patch

79 CCC Launch Site patch; note that the man on the insignia is being 'launched'

80 RT Lightning patch

81 RT Lightning variation: note that 213 indicates assignment to CCS, while 214 indicates assignment to CCN; possibly the team switched launch sites at some point

82 RT Louisiana patch

83 RT Louisiana variant

84 RT Louisiana variant

85 RT Maine patch; the inclusion of the word 'Airborne' is of some interest as teams were rarely inserted by parachute

86 RT Mamba patch; of interest is the inclusion of a submachine-gun on the patch rather than the M-16 or CAR-15 more commonly portrayed

87 RT Mike Facs patch; note that the patch is very similar to those for Command and Control sites; 'Facs' stands for Forward Area Cambodia Surveillance – in simple terms this team carried out cross-border ops into Cambodia

88 Mike Facs variant patch; note that the beret bears a Cambodian-style beret flash rather than the normal 5th SFG one

89 RT Minnesota patch; the mushroom cloud is of interest as normally it is only encountered on very unauthorized patches worn by Special Forces teams specializing in the use of tactical nuclear weapons, something it is doubtful RT Minnesota did in Southeast Asia

90 RT Mississippi patch

91 RT Missouri patch

92 Mobile Launch Team-1; this team was located at Phu Bai

93 Mobile Launch Team-2; this team was located at Quang Tri

94 RT Moccasin patch

95 RT Moccasin patch

96 RT Moccasin variant

97 FOB Monkey Mountain patch; this Forward Operating Base was located at Camp Fay

98 RT Montana patch

99 RT Nevada patch; note that the word 'Battle' is split; on locally made insignia misspellings or odd breaks in words were quite common because employees of local tailor shops sewing the insignia were copying a language they could not read or write

100 RT Nevada variation

101 RT New Hampshire patch; the presence of the bat is of interest as it is frequently associated with Provincial Recon Units – the direct action arm of the Phoenix Program; however it is also used to indicate skill in night operations

▶9th Infantry Division LRRP in Vietnam wears the black beret with locally made beret flash and LRRP tab, the LRRP arc over 9th Infantry Division subdued shoulder sleeve insignia, and locally made Recondo school patch on the pocket. (US Army)

PLATE 11

77

78

79

80

81

82

83

84

85

86

87

88

89

90

91

92

93

94

95

96

97

98

99

100

101

PLATE 12: MACV/SOG INSIGNIA CONTINUED

102 RT New Jersey patch; the Chinese characters mean 'Recon'

103 RT New Mexico patch; note that the poker hand is aces and eights, normally known as the 'Dead Man's Hand' because Wild Bill Hickock had this hand when killed. The Ace of Spades was often incorporated into insignia based on the idea that somehow this card was feared by the Communists. If true this is probably only because a few LRRP or other units used to leave Aces of Spades as 'calling cards' in the mouths of enemy killed

104 RT New York patch; the Grim Reaper was a fairly common icon on Vietnam insignia

105 RT North Carolina patch

106 RT Oregon patch

107 RT Pennsylvania patch

108 RT Plane patch

109 RT Plane shoulder tab

110 RT Prairie Fire patch; '18 Months North of the 17th Parallel' refers to the unit's mission in Laos

111 Laotian Expeditionary Force patch

112 RT Puerto Rico patch

113 RT Python patch

114 RT Rhode Island patch; note the presence once again of the Montagnard crossbow

115 RT Sidewinder patch

116 RT Sidewinder variation; note that 'Baru' is probably a misspelling of Bru, a Montagnard tribe

117 RT Spike patch

118 RT Tarantula patch

119 TL MACV patch

120 RT Texas shoulder tab

121 RT Texas patch

122 RT Trowell patch

123 RT Vermont patch

124 RT Viper patch

125 RT Viper variation

126 RT Virginia patch

▼Members of the 7th SFG (Airborne) undergoing winter guerrilla training. Note the early beret flash and insignia on the man in the right foreground. (US Army)

PLATE 12

102

103

104

105

106

107

108

109

110

111

112

113

114

115

116

117

118

119

120

121

122

123

124

125

126

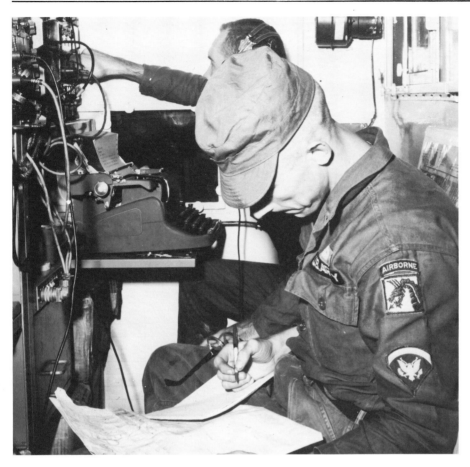

PLATE 13: MACV/SOG INSIGNIA CONTINUED

127 RT Washington patch
128 RT Washington shoulder tab
129 RT Wasp patch
130 RT Wasp variation
131 RT Weather patch
132 RT West Virginia patch; this very garish patch is one that best typifies the more colourful MACV/SOG insignia. The author has seen this insignia backed by both Vietnamese newspaper and camouflage material, both typically used in small tailor shops. The Chinese characters stand for 'Kill VC'
133 An unidentified recon team patch
134 Another unknown recon team patch
135 A Company, CCC Exploitation Force patch
136 Variation of A Company, CCC Exploitation Force
137 B Company, CCC Exploitation Force tab
138 C Company, CCC Exploitation Force patch
139 D Company, CCC Exploitation Force patch
140 1st Company, CCS Exploitation Force patch
141 RT Ohio patch
142 Cambodian Expeditionary Force Special Forces

Advisers patch; the Cambodian characters stand for 'Khymer National Number One Raiders'; 'Number One' was used throughout South-east Asia to mean the best
143 Forward Operations Base patch
144 Project Delta pocket patch
145 Project Sigma pocket patch
146 Military Assistance Command Vietnam/Joint Prisoner Resolution Center patch; this unit, which remained in Vietnam based at Tan Son Nhut long after MACV/SOG had ceased to operate, was theoretically involved in determining the fate of POW/MIAs but carried out other clandestine missions as well
147 Son Tay Raider patch; note that the insignia shows the lightning strike of the raid into and out of the camp
148 Son Tay Air Force elements patch; 'KITD/FOHS' refers to the fact that the Air Force support elements were not privy to much of the information about the raid; hence, 'Kept in the Dark/Fed Only Horse Shit'!
149 USARVITG pcoket Insignia
150 USARVITG subdued variation
151 Field Training Command pocket patch

PLATE 13

127

128

129

130

131

132

133

134

135

136

137

138

139

140

141

142

143

144

145

146

147

148

149

150

151

PLATE 14: COLOMBIA

Colombia's airborne forces came into existence with the formation of an airborne battalion in 1964. A parachute infantry battalion remains today based at Villavicencio. Additionally, within the army is a Lancero Battalion (equivalent to the US Rangers) and a Special Forces battalion. Among the approximately 1,500 Marines in Colombia are some airborne-qualified as well as a unit of combat swimmers.

Colombia's Lancero School is famous throughout Latin America for turning out tough jungle fighters. Located at the Colombian Army Infantry Centre at Tolemaida, the school gives one international course per year for students drawn from throughout Latin America. The school was originally established in 1955 to give specialized training to Colombian officers and NCOs. The course is divided into three phases. During Phase I (about six weeks) students learn to command small units and work on their physical training to prepare them for later phases. Phase II (about two weeks) involves field problems in rough terrain and adverse weather. Finally, Phase III (about two weeks) puts all the training together as students carry out small unit patrols and operations against aggressor forces.

1 Airborne beret badge
2 1st Airborne Battalion shoulder insignia and arc; note that normally Colombian infantry battalions are named after military heroes, but the airborne battalion is designated by its mission
3 1st Airborne Battalion shoulder insignia
4 Small pocket patch version of 1st Airborne Battalion insignia
5 Paratrooper shoulder arc
6 Cloth anti-guerrilla badge
7 Metal anti-guerrilla badge
8 Basic Special Forces qualification badge
9 Special Forces qualification badge in metal
10 Special Forces qualification badge in cloth
11 Arc worn by officers qualified as Lanceros, Commandos, parachutists
12 Lancero arc
13 Lancero pocket badge
14 Lancero shoulder insignia
15 Lancero School shoulder/pocket insignia
16 Lancero School graduate badge
17 Lancero School officer/instructor badge
18 Commando insignia
19 Commando de Selva qualification badge; this unit is composed of highly trained jungle fighters
20 Commando de Selva cloth insignia

PLATE 14 CONTINUED: BOLIVIA

Bolivia has a paratroop battalion, two Ranger Regiments, and three Andean Regiments. The Rangers were trained by the US Special Forces and helped track down Che Guevara. Bolivian special operations units are assigned to various divisions as follows: 5th Lanza Andean Regiment to the 1st Division; 17th Illimani Andean Regiment and 24th Mendez Arcos Ranger Regiment to the 2nd Division; 19th Murillo Andean Regiment and the Parachute Battalion to the 7th Division; 12th Manchego Ranger Regiment to the 8th Division. Bolivian paratroopers wear a black beret.

1 Airborne beret badge
2 Airborne shoulder patch
3 2nd Ranger Battalion
4 Company B, Airborne; Special Forces training class patch from 1972

PLATE 14

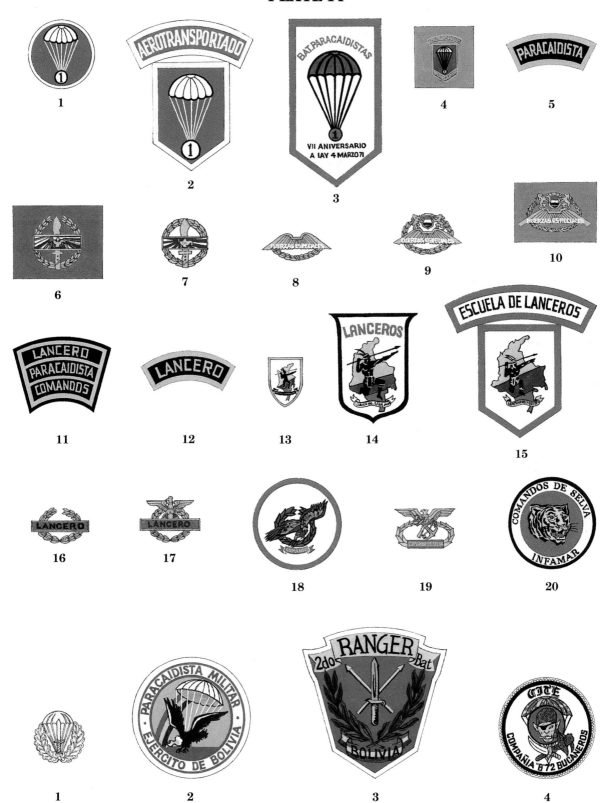

1

2

AEROTRANSPORTADO

3

BAT.PARACAIDISTAS

VII ANIVERSARIO
A IAY 4 MARZO 71

4

5

PARACAIDISTA

6

7

8

FUERZAS ESPEDALES

9

FUERZAS ESPECIALES

10

FUERZAS ESPECIALES

11

LANCERO
PARACAIDISTA
COMANDOS

12

LANCERO

13

14

LANCEROS

15

ESCUELA DE LANCEROS

16

LANCERO

17

LANCERO

18

COMANDO

19

COMANDO DE SELVA

20

COMANDOS DE SELVA

INFAMAR

1

2

PARACAIDISTA MILITAR
EJERCITO DE BOLIVIA

3

RANGER
2do   Bat

BOLIVIA

4

CITE
COMPAÑIA "B"72 BUCANEROS

35

PLATE 15: BRAZIL

Brazil's first airborne troops began training shortly after the Second World War and when sufficient numbers had qualified at the parachute school in Rio de Janeiro a parachute brigade was formed. From members of this brigade the Brazilian Special Forces were created in 1957. Currently, Brazilian Army airborne/SF units consist of the 1st Parachute Brigade at Rio; the 1st–5th Jungle Warfare Battalions (special operations units) with headquarters at Manaus; and the 2nd Parachute Brigade at Brasilia.

In 1957, a reconnaissance company was formed for the Brazilian Marines which also includes airborne/scuba-trained personnel. This unit has expanded to become the Toneleros Special Operations Battalion.

▲Very tough-looking Brazilian paratrooper illustrating the Brasil arc and airborne shoulder sleeve insignia. Also visible on the left breast are

Chilean and Venezuelan parachute brevets. On the right breast is what appears to be the jungle qualification badge. (Adrian Bohlen)

Brazilian jungle Commandos/special forces are trained at the Centro de Opracoes na Selva e Accoeo de Commandos at Manaus. Four courses per year in specialized jungle/Commando techniques for the Amazon region are taught at the centre. Among skills taught are demolitions, boobytraps, improvised landing fields, hydro and land navigation, mountain climbing, river crossing, survival, field medicine, jungle tactics, individual and small unit tactics. As can be seen, the course is quite similar to the US Ranger course.

1 Identification uncertain, but probably airborne beret badge
2 Same as No 1
3 Jungle Commando breast badge
4 Advanced army free-fall
5 Jungle Commando
6 Jungle Commando (gold is probably officer, silver NCO)
7 Cloth Jungle Commando badge
8 Expert Swimmer/Frogman
9 Brasil arc worn over parachute patch
10 Commandos arc
11 Special Forces arc
12 Airborne shoulder insignia
13 Jungle Commando School

PLATE 15 CONTINUED: CHILE

Chile's airborne forces trace their history to 1965 when the Army Parachute Battalion was formed as was the Parachute and Special Forces School at Peldehue. Currently this school offers the basic parachute course taking four weeks and including five jumps, jump-master, pathfinder, rigger, and Commando courses. Currently, a parachute battalion comes under the Air Force, while the Boinas Negras Special Forces/Commando Battalion comes under the Army. There are also combat swimmers assigned to the Chilean Marines. In addition to their black beret, Chilean Special Forces are marked by their Corvo (a curved jungle knife with which they are very proficient).

1 Commando/Special Forces qualification; note: this is the Corvo fighting knife
2 Unidentified
3 Parachute rigger
4 Commandos of the Special Forces Squadron
5 Variant of No 4
6 Special Forces
7 Special Forces breast badge
8 Commandos/Special Forces shoulder patch
9 Commandos shoulder patch
10 Another version of the Commando shoulder patch
11 Commando shoulder arc
12 Tiger (special forces?) shoulder arc

PLATE 15

1

2

3

4

5

6

7

8

9

10

11

12

13

1

2

3

4

5

6

7

8

9

10

11

12

37

PLATE 16: GUATEMALA

The first Guatemalan parachute company was formed in 1963, followed in 1967 by a special forces company, and in 1970 by another parachute company. In January 1971 these three units formed the 1st Parachute Battalion. In addition to this paratroop/special forces battalion, there is also a specialized counter-insurgency group with a special forces mission. The 1st Parachute Battalion is based at Base General Felipe Cruz about 65 miles south of Guatemala City. Many Guatemalan paratroopers have made combat jumps during the counter-insurgency war in that country. Members of the airborne units are identified by their black berets. Training includes five jumps for the basic parachute brevet, thirty jumps for expert, and 65 for master. As in US jump school, airborne training lasts three weeks.

1 Airborne beret badge

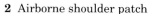

2 Airborne shoulder patch
3 1st Parachute Battalion shoulder patch
4 1st Parachute Company
5 Airborne shoulder tab
6 Subdued version of No 5
7 3rd Parachute Company (Type II)
8 3rd Parachute Company (Type I)
9 HQ Platoon, 3rd Parachute Company
10 1st Platoon, 3rd Parachute Company
11 2nd Platoon, 3rd Parachute Company
12 3rd Platoon, 3rd Parachute Company
13 4th Platoon, 3rd Parachute Company
14 Airborne Support Company
15 HQ Platoon, 1st Parachute Company
16 1st Platoon, 1st Parachute Company
17 2nd Platoon, 1st Parachute Company
18 3rd Platoon, 1st Parachute Company
19 4th Platoon, 1st Parachute Company

◄Guatemalan paratrooper offers a good view of that country's airborne beret badge as well as the basic parachute brevet. (*Soldier of Fortune* magazine)

PLATE 16

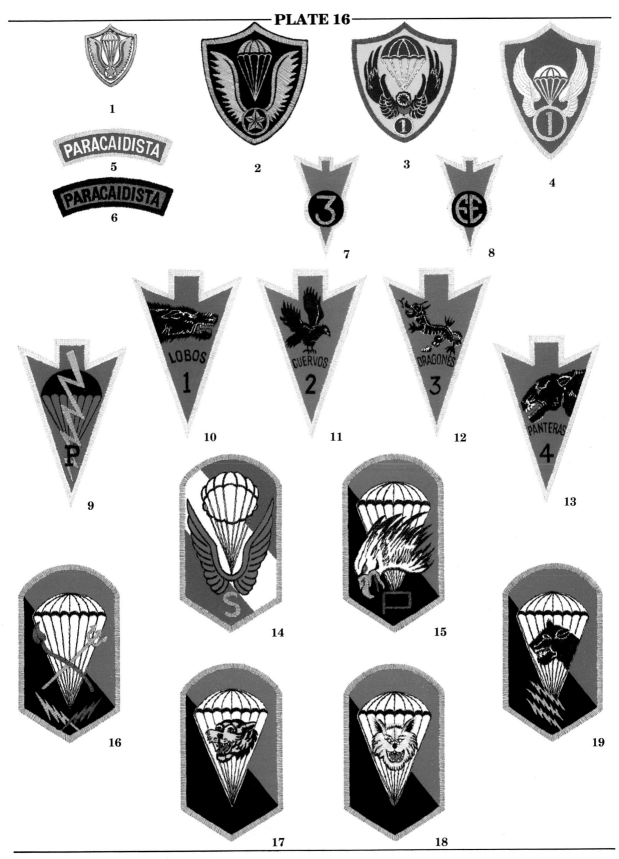

1

2

3

4

5 PARACAIDISTA

6 PARACAIDISTA

7

8

9

10

11

12

13

14

15

16

17

18

19

PLATE 17: GUATEMALA CONTINUED

20 2nd Parachute Company
21 HQ Platoon, 2nd Parachute Company
22 1st Platoon, 2nd Parachute Company
23 2nd Platoon, 2nd Parachute Company
24 3rd Platoon, 2nd Parachute Company
25 4th Platoon, 2nd Parachute Company

PLATE 17 CONTINUED: EL SALVADOR

El Salvador's first airborne company was formed in 1964. The current airborne battalion, though part of the Army, falls under Air Force control. There are also two special forces groups. Parachute training lasts four weeks, during which six jumps are made. Until 1983, airborne troops wore a dark-blue beret, possibly because of their association with the Air Force, but since that time they have worn a maroon beret.

1 Officers' airborne collar insignia
2 Other ranks' airborne collar insignia
3 Airborne Commando Group
4 1st Airborne Squadron
5 2nd Airborne Squadron
6 HQ (Reserve) Platoon
7 Airborne Weapons Platoon
8 1st Airborne Platoon
9 2nd Airborne Platoon
10 3rd Airborne Platoon

PLATE 17

ASIA

PLATE 18: INDONESIA

Few if any countries can match Indonesia in its diversity of airborne/élite units. Shortly after Independence, Indonesia formed various parachute and parachute raider battalions until, in 1952, the Para-Commando Regiment was formed. This unit, RPKAD, includes not just parachute-qualified but also amphibious-qualified personnel. By 1976 the RPKAD had expanded to two brigades – the 17th and 18th – as well as four independent para-raider battalions. Additionally, there's a separate special forces command, known as KOPASSANDHA, which has two Para-Commando groups. Combat jumps were made by members of the Para-Commandos in 1958 on Sumatra and in 1962 on new Guinea.

Other units which included parachute personnel are the Indonesian Marines, part of whom are the KIPAM combat swimmers; the Air Force Quick Reaction Forces (KOPASGAT); and the National Police Mobile Brigade (PELIPOR).

This diversity required a number of training establishments. The army actually runs two schools, one in the Cimahi area near Bandung, Java, and another at Ujung Pandang, Sulawesi. Four parachute schools operate at Cimahi – Para Commando/Special Forces, Army Strategic Command (KOSTRAD), Raider, and Airborne Infantry. The Air Force operates its own school at Sulaiman Air Base at Bandung, Java. The Marines operate two schools – for Western forces at Jakarta, Java, and for Eastern forces at Surabaya, Java. The National Police run their school at Borong, Java. Various levels of parachute badge including free-fall are awarded to each of the services.

Berets are worn by the various élite units as follows: Special Forces/Commando red, Army Strategic Command light-green, Airborne Infantry dark-green, Air Force Rapid Reaction Force orange, Marine Paras violet, National Police Mobile Brigade dark-blue (almost black). In addition, Army Raiders wear a distinctive camo cap instead of a beret.

1 Cloth Parachute Commando qualification badge
2 Parachute Commando shoulder sleeve insignia
3 Commando shoulder arc
4 Variation of the Commando shoulder arc
5 Parachute Commando shoulder title
6 Unidentified
7 Cloth Parachute Commando qualification badge
8 Variation of the Parachute Commando qualification
9 Raider qualification badge in cloth
10 Unidentified
11 Airborne shoulder title
12 Airborne shoulder sleeve insignia
13 Metal Parachute Commando qualification badge
14 Metal Parachute Commando qualification badge
15 Raider qualification badge
16 Parachute Commando qualification badge
17 Unidentified
18 Metal Airborne badge
19 Commando qualification badge
20 Airborne shoulder sleeve insignia
21 Airborne shoulder sleeve insignia
22 Parachute Raider shoulder sleeve insignia
23 Raider shoulder sleeve insignia
24 Commando shoulder sleeve insignia
25 Raider shoulder title
26 Raider shoulder sleeve insignia
27 Commando shoulder sleeve insignia
28 Raider shoulder arc
29 Commando shoulder sleeve insignia

PLATE 18

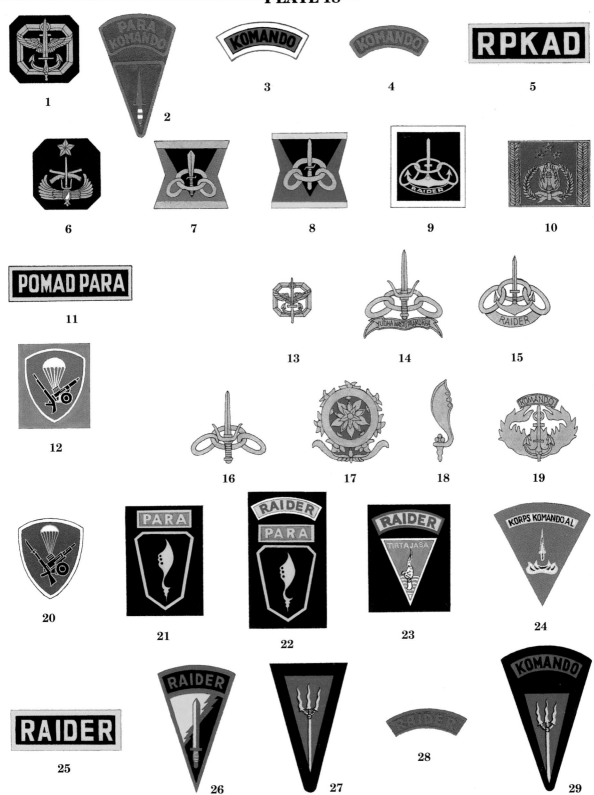

1

2

3

4

5

6

7

8

9

10

POMAD PARA

11

13

14

15

12

16

17

18

19

20

21

22

23

24

RAIDER

25

26

27

28

29

PLATE 19: REPUBLIC OF VIETNAM

The first Viet parachute unit was the 1st Indo-Chinese Parachute Company, formed in 1948 as part of the French colonial forces. Soon, Indo-Chinese parachute companies were attached to many of the French parachute battalions serving in Indo-China. Many of these companies were expanded to battalion strength, forming the basis for the Vietnamese Airborne Group after the French withdrawal. In 1959 this unit was re-designated the Airborne Brigade, then in 1965 the Airborne Division.

The Vietnamese Special Forces (the LLDB) were originally formed in 1958 as the Joint Operations Group expanding to the 31st and 77th Special Observation Battalions in 1959. As the Civilian Irregular Defense Group Program grew so did the number of LLDB Groups as the 81st, 606th and 660th were added. After the re-deployment of US Special Forces to the USA in 1971, the LLDB was re-organized into the 81st Special Airborne Battalion to carry out special ops within South Vietnam, the Liaison Office (which absorbed much of MACV/SOG's duties), and the Technical Directorate which carried out missions into North Vietnam.

Generally considered the best of South Vietnam's élite units were the Biet Dong Quan, the Viet Rangers. The ARVN Rangers were first formed in 1960 and initially served in company-strength units, later expanded to battalion strength. In 1967, the Rangers were organized into groups and became each corps tactical zone's primary reaction element. The Ranger Training Centre at Duc My was probably the best training facility within the entire ARVN structure. After the US Special Forces handed over the CIDG program to the Vietnamese, many of the most effective CIDG troops became ARVN Rangers.

Other Vietnamese troops trained for airborne/special operations included the MIKE Forces which were élite light infantry, often airborne-qualified, used as reaction forces directly under US Special Forces control. Also highly effective were the Provincial Recon Units, which included some airborne-trained troops and many turned VC formed into the 'teeth' units of the Phoenix Program. Within the Viet Marines were highly trained personnel including some with a recon mission. Finally, the Vietnamese Navy had their own combat swimmer unit, the LDNN, similar to US Navy SEALs.

Vietnamese airborne troops wore the red beret; ARVN Rangers wore a maroon beret. Perhaps the best-known ARVN Ranger headgear, however, was the steel helmet with their Black Panther insignia painted on the helmet or the camo cover. LLDB wore green berets similar to their US advisers. PRUs wore different coloured berets depending on the province. Black, red, and green were most common.

1 Metal Airborne beret badge
2 Bullion Airborne beret badge
3 Cloth Airborne beret badge
4 Airborne Group shoulder sleeve insignia
5 Another version of the Airborne Group SSI; note colour similarities to the British Parachute Regiment
6 Airborne Brigade SSI
7 Airborne Division SSI
8 Cloth jump status indicator badge
9 Metal jump status indicator badge
10 Unidentified
11 2nd Parachute Medical Battalion cloth pocket crest
12 1st Parachute Medical Battalion cloth
13 3rd Parachute Medical Battalion cloth
14 1st Parachute Battalion metal
15 2nd Parachute Battalion metal
16 3rd Parachute Battalion metal
17 5th Parachute Battalion metal
18 6th Parachute Battalion metal
19 7th Parachute Battalion metal
20 8th Parachute Battalion metal
21 9th Parachute Battalion metal
22 11th Parachute Battalion metal; note: for the Vietnamese the number '10' meant 'the worst', hence the lack of a battalion so designated
23 Parachute Artillery Battalion
24 Parachute Medical Battalion
25 1st Parachute Battalion silk

PLATE 19

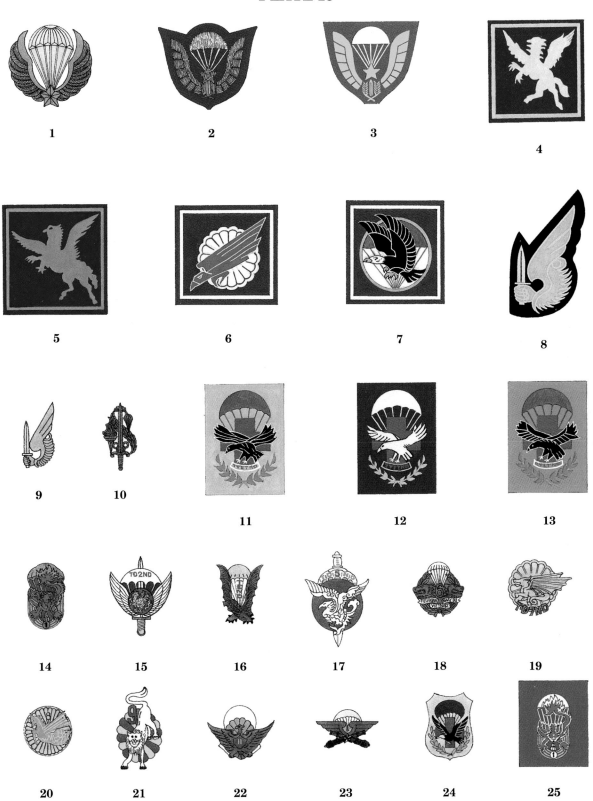

1

2

3

4

5

6

7

8

9

10

11

12

13

14

15

16

17

18

19

20

21

22

23

24

25

PLATE 20: REPUBLIC OF VIETNAM AIRBORNE AND RANGER

26 2nd Parachute Battalion silk
27 3rd Parachute Battalion silk
28 5th Parachute Battalion silk
29 6th Parachute Battalion silk
30 7th Parachute Battalion silk
31 8th Parachute Battalion silk
32 9th Parachute Battalion silk
33 11th Parachute Battalion silk
34 Parachute Artillery Battalion silk
35 Parachute Engineer Battalion silk
36 Parachute Medical Battalion silk
37 Parachute Signal Battalion silk
38 Parachute Support Battalion silk
39 Unidentified
40 Unidentified

1 Ranger branch insignia
2 Ranger beret badge
3 Ranger pocket insignia
4 Ranger breast qualification badge, metal
5 Ranger breast qualification badge, cloth
6 Ranger breast qualification badge, cloth, subdued
7 Ranger breast qualification badge, variation on camouflage; note, there are numerous cloth variations of this badge, manufactured in local areas of Vietnam, often sewn directly on to uniforms
8 Ranger Tab
9 Ranger Tab

▼ Good view of the ARVN airborne beret badge (left) and the 5th Special Forces Group (Airborne) beret badge (right). (US Army)

PLATE 20

26

27

28

29

30

31

32

33

34

35

36

37

38

39

40

1

2

3

4

8

9

5

6

7

PLATE 21: REPUBLIC OF VIETNAM RANGERS

10 Ranger arc; note, on Ranger tabs and arcs, the colour normally indicates which of the four tactical zones the Rangers were assigned to as follows: Green-I, Red-II, Maroon-III. and Yellow-IV
11 Another version of the Ranger arc
12 Ranger arc/Border Defense (Border Defense Rangers helped interdict infiltration routes)
13 US Ranger adviser arc for the Duc My Ranger Training Centre
14 US Ranger adviser arc for the Ranger High Command
15 US Ranger adviser arc for III Corps Rangers
16 US Ranger adviser arc for the 34th Ranger Battalion
17 US Ranger adviser arc for the 41st Ranger Battalion
18 US Ranger adviser arc for the 30th Ranger Battalion
19 US Ranger adviser arc for the TNF Company
20 Border Defense arc
21 Border Defense arc (subdued)
22 Reconnaissance arc
23 Special Reconnaissance Infiltration arc
24 Ranger arc
25 Reconnaissance arc
26 Reconnaissance arc
27 Reconnaissance scroll
28 Reconnaissance scroll
29 Bing Long Province arc
30 Ranger tab; note, normally on these tabs the colour indicates province as discussed above, the boxed number at left indicates the battalion or team; for example, this tab is for 33rd Ranger Group Administration based in III Corps
31 32nd Battalion 2nd Ranger Group
32 21st Battalion, 1st Ranger Group
33 77th Ranger Battalion
34 23rd Battalion, 2nd Ranger Group
35 96th Battalion, 21st Ranger Group
36 23rd Battalion, 2nd Ranger Group
37 Command and Service Group, 3rd Ranger Group
38 52nd Battalion, 3rd Ranger Group
39 5th Ranger Battalion
40 30th Battalion, 5th Ranger Group
41 Artillery, 32nd Ranger Group

▲Vietnamese Ranger officer shows the ARVN Ranger qualification badge on the right breast. (Society of Vietnamese Rangers)

PLATE 21

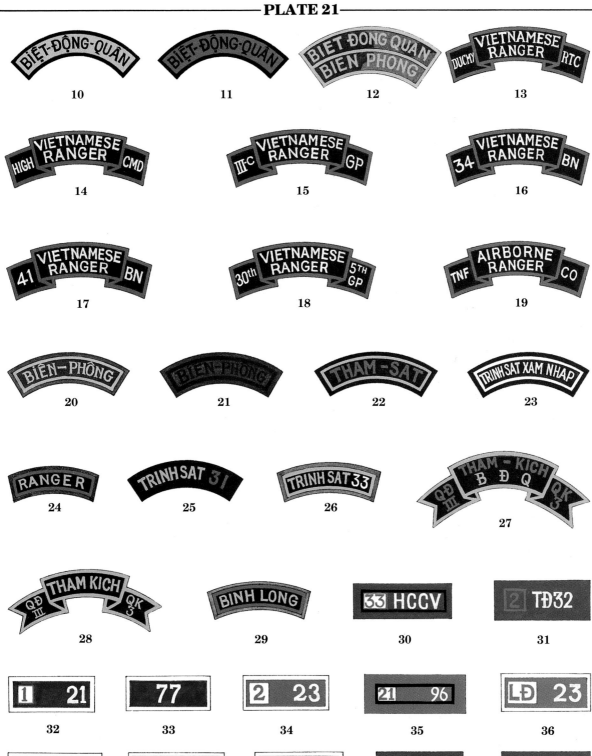

10

11

12

13

14

15

16

17

18

19

20

21

22

23

24

25

26

27

28

29

30

31

32

33

34

35

36

37

38

39

40

41

PLATE 22: REPUBLIC OF VIETNAM RANGERS

42 7th Ranger Group
43 Radar, 7th Ranger Group
44 85th Battalion, 7th Ranger Group
45 7th Ranger Group
46 7th Ranger Group
47 86th Ranger Battalion
48 41st Ranger Battalion, 4th Ranger Group
49 44th Ranger Battalion, 4th Ranger Group shoulder slide
50 42nd Ranger Battalion, 4th Ranger Group shoulder slide
51 Ranger shoulder insignia and small distinctive insignia version
52 Unidentified
53 Ranger Training Centre pocket insignia
54 Cambodian Expedition pocket insignia
55 Ranger Unit pocket insignia
56 BDQ (Ranger) pocket or shoulder insignia
57 Ranger pocket insignia (subdued)
58 Ranger pocket insignia (semi-subdued)
59 33rd Ranger Group Artillery tab and insignia
60 35th Ranger Battalion tab and insignia
61 3rd Ranger Group tab and insignia
62 31st Ranger Battalion, 3rd Ranger Group tab and insignia
63 38th Ranger Battalion, 5th Ranger Group tab and insignia
64 7th Ranger Group tab and insignia
65 Ranger Group communications
66 Ranger administration
67 Variant Ranger pocket insignia
68 Variant Ranger pocket insignia ('Sat Cong' means 'Kill Communists')

◀At the ARVN Ranger training centre a Vietnamese instructor and his American counterpart wear maroon BDQ berets with the Ranger beret and badge. The American also wears the Ranger pocket patch. (US Army)

PLATE 22

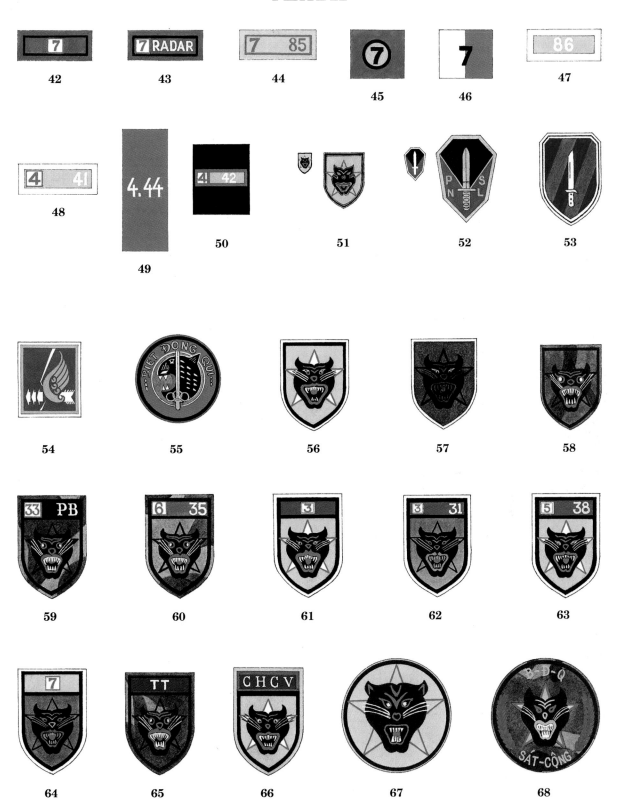

42

43

44

45

46

47

48

49

50

51

52

53

54

55

56

57

58

59

60

61

62

63

64

65

66

67

68

PLATE 23: REPUBLIC OF VIETNAM RANGERS

69 Reconnaissance Force pocket insignia
70 Old-style III Corps Ranger insignia
71 Subdued version of No. 74
72 III Corps Reconnaissance pocket insignia
73 II Corps Reconnaissance pocket insignia
74 II Corps Ranger pocket insignia
75 3rd Sector, III Corps Ranger pocket insignia
76 Ranger Reconnaissance pocket insignia
77 Ranger Reconnaissance pocket insignia
78 Ranger pocket insignia
79 71st Border Defense Ranger Battalion
80 74th Ranger Battalion
81 23rd Ranger Battalion Reconnaissance pocket insignia
82 33rd Ranger Group Administration tab and pocket insignia
83 11th Ranger Battalion pocket insignia; Vietnamese phrase at top translates as 'To have the courage to win'
84 33rd Ranger Battalion pocket insignia
85 Variation of No. 84
86 Another variation of No. 84
87 41st Ranger Battalion pocket insignia; note that unlike most Ranger insignia which use the leopard, this insignia incorporates the Ranger beret badge
88 74th Ranger Battalion shoulder loop
89 91st Ranger Battalion (Airborne); note the inclusion of the parachute – not all ARVN Rangers were airborne-qualified
90 Reconnaissance pocket insignia
91 Special Reconnaissance pocket insignia
92 Airborne Reconnaissance pocket insignia
93 Unidentified Reconnaissance Unit; Vietnamese phrase translates as 'Ready to die'

▼Vietnamese paratroopers (note the shoulder sleeve insignia on the soldier in the right foreground) undergo survival training with the 1st Special Forces Group. (US Army)

PLATE 23

69

70

71

72

73

74

75

76

77

78

79

80

81

82

83

84

85

86

87

88

89

90

91

92

93

PLATE 24: REPUBLIC OF VIETNAM SPECIAL FORCES

1 LLDB original beret badge
2 Final version of LLDB beret badge in bullion
3 Final LLDB beret badge in cloth
4 Joint Observation Battalion
5 31st Special Forces Battalion
6 77th Special Forces Battalion
7 606th Special Forces Battalion
8 660th Special Forces Battalion
9 LLDB pocket insignia
10 Variant of No. 9
11 Variant of No. 9
12 Subdued version of No. 9
13 Airborne Ranger ('Nhay Du' means airborne); this patch was always known as the 'Tony the Tiger' patch after the breakfast cereal character
14 77th Special Forces Battalion (phrase at top translates as 'Honour and Gallantry')
15 81st Special Forces Group
16 81st Special Forces Group strike company
17 81st Special Forces Group Intelligence unit
18 81st Special Forces Battalion pocket insignia
19 I.D. not certain, but probably a variant 81st Special Forces Battalion insignia

20 81st Special Forces Battalion variant of No. 18
21 81st Special Forces Battalion Lightning Force
22 81st Special Forces Battalion Reconnaissance Force
23 Technical Directorate
24 Technical Directorate variant
25 Technical Directorate variant
26 Technical Directorate variant
27 Technical Directorate; note the depiction of the coffin – missions carried out by this unit were often considered suicide missions; Vietnamese phrase translates as 'Honour Nation'
28 Technical Directorate (Vietnamese phrase translates as 'Invisible Boundary')
29 Liaison Office
30 Command and Control Central (Chinese letters translate as 'Reconnaissance')
31 Reconnaissance Team Loi Ho
32 Task Force 1
33 Command and Control South

▼Member of the Viet Special Forces, the LLDB, in the centre, wears the green beret with the later version of the LLDB beret badge. (US Army)

PLATE 24

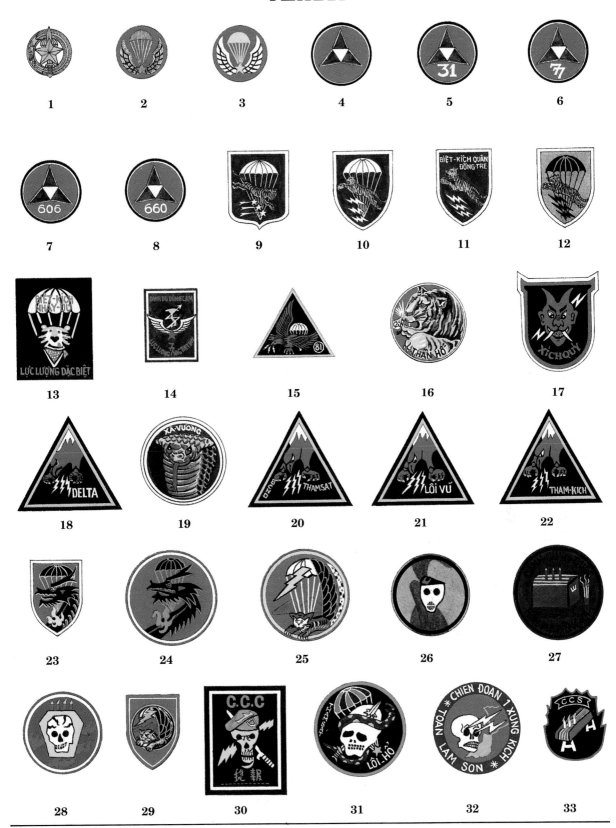

1

2

3

4

5

6

7

8

9

10

11

12

13

14

15

16

17

18

19

20

21

22

23

24

25

26

27

28

29

30

31

32

33

PLATE 25: REPUBLIC OF VIETNAM

34 Reconnaissance Team Truong Son
35 Liaison Office Exploitation Force
36 Exploitation Force ('Tham-Tu' means 'suicide')
37 235th Exploitation Force (exploitation forces were rapidly inserted into an area when reconnaissance forces encountered the enemy)
38 Exploitation Force ('BD Tap Kich' means 'Special Raiding Force')
39 Exploitation Force (Border Force)
40 Lang Thanh Training School
41 Unknown reconnaissance/exploitation force; 'Quyet To' means 'Ready to Die'
42 Same as No. 41
43 Buon Mi Ga Mobile Guerrilla Force
44 Buon Sar Pa Mobile Guerrilla Force; note the bow which normally indicates a Montagnard unit
45 E. Pul Blar Wang Mobile Guerrilla Force
46 Rhade Mobile Guerrilla Force (The Rhade were the largest Montagnard tribe)
47 Koho Mobile Guerrilla Force
48 Darlac Province Mobile Guerrilla Force
49 5th Mobile Strike Force Command
50 Camp Strike Force
51 C-1 MIKE Force
52 C-2 MIKE Force
53 Mobile Strike Force
54 C-1 MIKE Reaction Force
55 3rd MIKE Force Battalion, II Corps
56 C-3 MIKE Force
57 C-4 MIKE Force
58 C-4 MIKE Force
59 Mobile Strike Force pocket patch
60 Eagle Flight (Eagle Flights were quick reaction forces prior to the formation of the MIKE Forces)
61 Mobile Strike Force
62 Mobile Strike Force
63 Mobile Strike Force
64 Mobile Strike Force (Vietnamese phrase translates as, 'Honourable Death Rather than a Shameful Life')
65 Duc Lap Civilian Irregular Defense Group
66 CIDG Tay Ninh Province
67 Reconnaissance Teams
68 Nung Security Detachment; (The Nungs were ethnic Chinese who made excellent soldiers. Because of their loyalty, US Special Forces normally used them as special security forces at SF installations)

▼General Westmoreland and Secretary of Defense McNamara inspect Vietnamese troops including the airborne trooper in the left foreground who offers a good view of the bullion airborne beret badge. (US Army)

PLATE 25

34

35

36

37

38

39

40

41

42

43

44

45

46

47

48

49

50

51

52

53

54

55

56

57

58

59

60

61

62

63

64

65

66

67

68

PLATE 26: REPUBLIC OF VIETNAM

69 Provincial Reconnaissance Unit pocket insignia (the PRUs were mercenaries, in many cases turned Communists, and provided the 'teeth' for the Phoenix Program)
70 Another PRU insignia
71 Tay Ninh Province PRU
72 Bien Hoa Province PRU
73 Phong Dinh Province PRU
74 Bien Thuan Province PRU
75 Binh Tuy Province PRU
76 Kien Giang Province PRU
77 Kien Hoa Province PRU
78 Phuoc Lang Province PRU
79 Quang Nam Province PRU

80 Quang Ngai Province PRU
81 Quang Tri Province PRU
82–84 Unidentified PRUs
85–89 LDNN (Vietnamese SEAL) breast badges. The different colours outlining the scuba gear identified the sub-units
90 Another version of the LDNN qualification badge
91 LDNN pocket patch
92 Another version of the LDNN pocket patch
93 Explosive Ordnance Disposal pocket patch
94 LDNN pocket patch

▼Vietnamese parachutists serving in the French Army during the Indo-China War sport jaunty maroon berets and French parachute brevets on the distinctive French camo jump smock. (ECP)

PLATE 26

69

70

71

72

73

74

75

76

77

78

79

80

81

82

83

84

85

86

87

88

89

90

91

92

93

94

PLATE 27: CAMBODIA

The history of Cambodia's élite units roughly parallels that of Vietnam in that the original parachute and Commando units were formed as part of the French colonial forces in Indo-China. As the counter-insurgency war in South-east Asia engulfed Cambodia as well, that country's élite light infantry forces expanded to include airborne, special forces, *choc* (shock), and Commando troops. By 1970, there were two parachute brigades – the 1st and 2nd – with seven parachute battalions. Because the US Special Forces worked closely with Cambodian élite forces throughout the 1960s and 1970s and because at least some Cambodian special operations personnel were trained in Vietnam, there will be many similarities with US/Viet élite insignia.

1 Airborne beret badge
2 Special Forces beret badge
3 Crossed arrows and dagger would indicate this is a Special Forces flash and beret badge
4 Airborne reconnaissance brevet
5 Airborne collar insignia
6 Cloth collar insignia
7 Special Forces shoulder insignia; note the influence of the US Special Forces insignia
8 Another version of the Special Forces SSI
9 Reconnaissance Team cap badge
10 Training detachment scroll, perhaps worn by US personnel
11 Airborne shoulder insignia and arc
12 Another airborne shoulder insignia
13 Airborne HQ
14 1st Parachute Brigade
15 3rd Airborne Battalion
16 Airborne Reconnaissance Teams
17 Probably airborne maintenance detachment
18 Unidentified
19 Possibly 21st *Bataillon de Choc*
20 Possibly 103rd *Bataillon de Choc*
21 Possibly 205th *Bataillon de Choc*
22 Medium Range Reconnaissance pocket patch
23 Unidentified reconnaissance unit
24 701st *Bataillon de Choc*
25 68th *Bataillon de Choc*
26 3rd Infantry Division Reconnaissance
27 20th *Bataillon de Choc*

◀ *The effectiveness of good camouflage is well demonstrated in this illustration. The year is 1975, and we see members of the 1st Parachute Brigade, well armed, ready to break cover in fighting around the suburbs of Pnom Penh.*

PLATE 27

1   2   3   4   5   6   7

8   9   10   11   12

13   14   15   16   17

18   19   20   21   22

23   24   25   26   27

PLATE 28: CAMBODIA

28 Reconnaissance pocket patch
29 1st Infantry Division Reconnaissance
30 Mid Range Reconnaissance Patrol pocket patch
31 4th *Bataillon de Choc*
32 86th *Bataillon de Choc*
33 46th *Bataillon de Choc*
34 53rd *Bataillon de Choc*
35 10th *Bataillon de Choc*
36 197th *Bataillon de Choc*
37 285th *Bataillon de Choc*
38 317th *Bataillon de Choc*

39 319th *Bataillon de Choc*
40 324th *Bataillon de Choc*
41 509th *Bataillon de Choc*
42 524th *Bataillon de Choc*
43 537th *Bataillon de Choc*
44 537th *Bataillon de Choc*
45 606th *Bataillon de Choc*
46 607th *Bataillon de Choc*
47 Unidentified
48 Unidentified
49 Unidentified
50 Unidentified
51 Unidentified

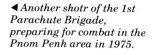

◀*Another shotr of the 1st Parachute Brigade, preparing for combat in the Pnom Penh area in 1975.*

PLATE 28

28

29

30

31

32

33

34

35

36

37

38

39

40

41

42

43

44

45

46

47

48

49

50

51

PLATE 29: TAIWAN

Under the OSS, various parachute-trained Chinese units were formed during the Second World War. Then, after the war's end, a Parachute Corps was formed within the Nationalist forces, based upon parachute Commando units trained during the war. Parachute units remained among those which fled to Taiwan as the Communists seized power. Among these were Intelligence operatives with parachute training used to infiltrate the mainland. Also formed in 1958 was the 1st Special Forces Group of about 2,500 men. It was followed over the next few years by the 2nd, 3rd, and 4th SF Groups. Currently, Taiwan still fields these four Special Forces Groups as well as the 1st and 2nd Airborne Battle Groups (Brigades) of the Army. Special Long Range Amphibious Reconnaissance teams and both Army and Marine combat swimmers also exist.

1 Dragons Parachute Team pocket patch
2 Iron Men Parachute Team pocket patch
3 Variation of the Iron Men pocket patch
4 Special Forces pocket patch
5 Special Forces pocket patch, possibly parachute team
6 Special Forces pocket patch
7 Special Forces assigned to the 4th Division
8 Special Forces rough terrain unit
9 Special Forces rough terrain variant
10 Special Forces rough terrain unit
11–15 Special Forces patches; note the arrowhead of the US Special Forces which helped train the Taiwan SF; colours probably indicate different battalions since each group has five battalions
16 Unidentified
17 Unknown but possibly aerial delivery unit
18 Variant of No. 17
19 Variant of No. 17
20 Unidentified airborne unit
21 Airborne pocket patch
22 Special Forces Special Training Detachment
23 Variant of No. 22
24 Variant of No. 22
25 Political Warfare Commando unit assigned to the off-shore front

PLATE 29

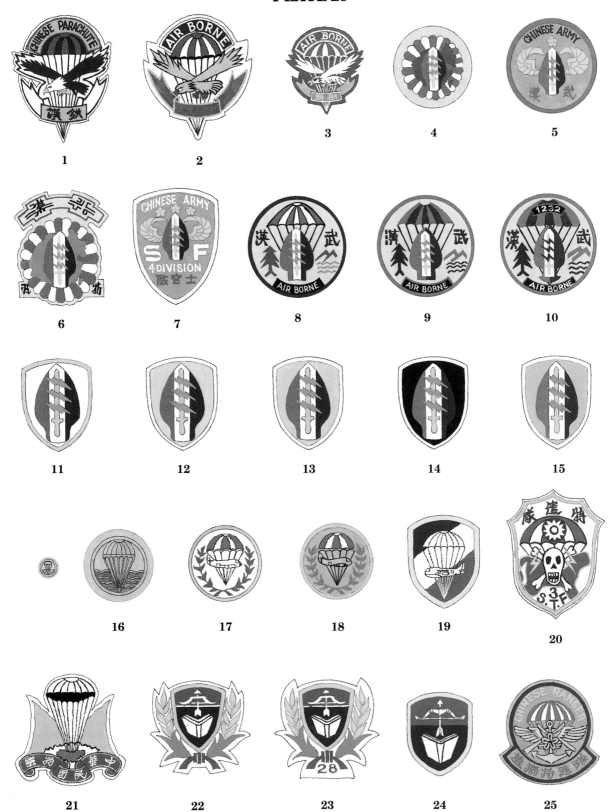

1

2

3

4

5

6

7

8

9

10

11

12

13

14

15

16

17

18

19

20

21

22

23

24

25

PLATE 30: TAIWAN

26 Off-shore Commando unit
27 Off-shore Commando unit
28 Off-shore Commando unit
29 Commando
30 Commando
31 Commando
32 Commando
33 Commando
34 Commando
35 Divisional Commando
36 Divisional Commando
37 Divisional Commando
38 Commando
39 Commando
40 Long Range Amphibious Reconnaissance
41 Marine Combat Swimmer
42 Navy Commando, Matsu Islands
43 Army Commando, Kinman Island
44 Unidentified, probably scuba/amphibious unit
45 Unidentified, probably scuba/amphibious unit
46 Scuba pocket patch
47 LRRP Team badge
48 Amphibious Reconnaissance Team badge
49 Scuba Team badge
50 Special Forces Scuba

PLATE 30

26

27

28

29

30

31

32

33

34

35

36

37

38

39

40

41

42

43

44

45

46

47

48

49

50

PLATE 31: TAIWAN

51 Army Scuba
52 Underwater Demolition; Note, this patch is very similar to those used by US Navy SEAL and UDT units
53 Underwater Demolition Team 2
54 UDT
55 Army Combat Swimmer
56 Unidentified, possibly Chinese Marines Amphibious Raider
57 Unidentified, possibly Amphibious Raider
58 Marine Commando, junk force raider units
59 Unidentified, possibly Amphibious Raider
60 Unidentified, possibly Amphibious Raider

61 Marine Commando, junk force raider
62 Marine Commando, junk force raider
63 Marine Amphibious Raider
64 Army Commando arc
65 Navy Commando arc
66–68 Off-shore Commando arcs
69 Special Forces sniper arc
70 Commando arc
71 Special Forces arc
72 HALO team
73 HALO
74 Sky Diver Team
75 HALO

PLATE 31

51

52

53

54

55

56

57

58

59

60

61

62

63

64

65

66

67

68

69

70

71

72

73

74

75

PLATE 32: REPUBLIC OF KOREA

South Korea's first parachute troops were those assigned to the United Nations Partisans in Korea during the Korean War. This was a guerrilla unit which operated in North Korea for raiding and Intelligence gathering. Later the ROK Army included 1st and 5th Parachute Brigades as well as Special Forces units. Korean Special Forces personnel, who wear a distinctive black beret, served in Vietnam. In the mid 1970s, Korean Ranger units and the two airborne brigades were converted to Special Forces Brigades. In addition to the Special Warfare HQ and Command there are the 1st, 3rd, 5th, 7th, 9th, 11th and 13th Special Forces Brigades. At the Special Warfare School near Seoul parachute, HALO, scuba, and other specialized training is given. Ranger training is given by individual units and at the ROK Infantry School. Each Infantry Division has a Reconnaissance Battalion members of which are normally Airborne- and Ranger-qualified. Other airborne-qualified units include the ROK Marine Reconnaissance Battalion, Navy Combat Swimmers (UDT), and Air Force Combat Control and Pararescue.

1 Special Forces beret badge
2 Variant of No. 1
3 Parachute School distinctive insignia
4 1st Parachute Brigade distinctive insignia
5 1st Parachute Brigade
6 1st Parachute Brigade
7 5th Airborne Battalion
8 Unidentified airborne unit
9 Probably 5th Parachute Brigade
10 Airborne Brigade HQ
11 Unidentified, possibly old-style 1st Special Forces Brigade
12 Unidentified, probably old-style 9th Special Forces Brigade
13 Special Warfare Centre
14 1st Special Forces Brigade
15 3rd Special Forces Brigade
16 5th Special Forces Brigade
17 7th Special Forces Brigade
18 9th Special Forces Brigade
19 11th Special Forces Brigade
20 13th Special Forces Brigade
21 Basic Ranger qualification
22 Advanced Ranger qualification
23 Ranger cloth
24 Ranger cloth variant

PLATE 32

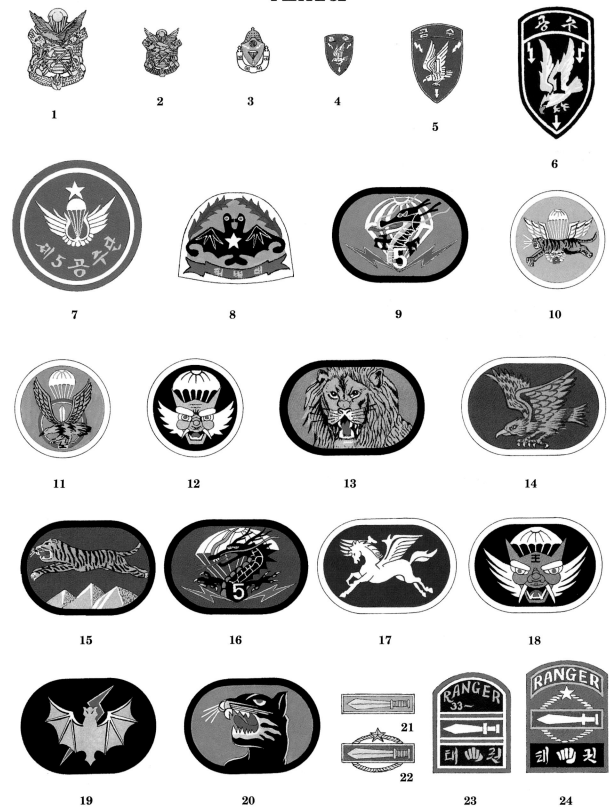

1

2

3

4

5

6

7

8

9

10

11

12

13

14

15

16

17

18

19

20

21

22

23

24

PLATE 33: REPUBLIC OF KOREA

25 Airborne Ranger
26 Marine Corps Airborne Ranger
27 Marine Corps Airborne Ranger variant
28 Ranger
29 Unidentified
30 Ranger variant
31 Marine UDT
32 Army UDT
33 Marine Combat Swimmer
34 Unidentified Combat Swimmer
35 Scuba detachment
36 Parachute Amphibious Reconnaissance

37 Senior Parachute Amphibious Reconnaissance
38 Master Parachute Amphibious Reconnaissance
39 Marine Senior Parachute Amphibious Reconnaissance
40 Marine Master Amphibious Reconnaisance: note, symbols on insignia indicate that qualifications include airborne, Ranger, small boat
41 Marine Senior Amphibious Reconnaissance variant
42 Basic Marine Amphibious Reconnaissance
43 Basic Marine Amphibious Reconnaissance without airborne wings
44 Amphibious Reconnaissance pocket patch

◄Republic of Korea Special Forces soldier wearing the black beret and beret badge. (US Army)

PLATE 33

26

27

28

29

25

30

31

32

33

35

36

34

37

38

39

40

41

42

43

44

MIDDLE EAST

PLATE 34: IRAN

Under the Shah, the Iranians fielded an Airborne Brigade – the 25th – and a Special Forces Brigade as well as specialized mountain Commandos. Many of these units were decimated during the revolution and the war with Iraq, but enough remained to carry out special operations, with the Revolutionary Guards, during the fighting. Iranian Special Forces had also seen action beside the British SAS in Oman. Like the US Special Forces who trained them, Iranian Special Forces traditionally have worn the green beret.

1 Airborne beret badge
2 Another form of the airborne beret badge

3 Airborne shoulder sleeve insignia
4 Another version of the airborne shoulder sleeve insignia
5 Unidentified shoulder sleeve insignia, possibly Ranger or special forces
6 Ranger badge
7 Mountain Ranger badge
8 Special Forces insignia showing the influence of US Special Forces training teams
9 Variation of the Ranger insignia
10 Another Ranger insignia, possibly of Ranger-qualified members of the Royal Guard
11 Special Forces insignia
12 Special Forces insignia

◀ Iranian Special Forces trooper offers view of the Iranian SF badge.

PLATE 34 CONTINUED: ISRAEL

Israel's first parachute unit was formed in 1948. Since then the paratroops have acted as élite shock infantry in each of Israel's wars, though the only two combat jumps came during the 1956 war. This first airborne unit was designated the 890th Parachute Battalion, but in 1954 it was amalgamated with Unit 101, a cross-border raiding unit, to become Unit 202 and eventually the 202nd Parachute Brigade. A reserve brigade was soon added to create a Parachute Corps. By the 1980s

1 Infantry beret badge, worn by paratroopers on their red berets
2 Airborne Commando
3 Aerial Delivery
4 Airborne Engineers
5 Rigger
6 Free-fall paratroop
7 Unidentified
8 35th Parachute Brigade arm shield
9 Parachute School arm shield
10 Commando qualification badge

PLATE 34

1

2

3

4

5

6

7

8

9

10

11

12

1

2

3

4

5

6

7

8

9

10

there were five parachute brigades in existence – 8th, 13th, 29th, 31st and 35th.

Special reconnaissance units known as 'Sayaret' function as LRRPs within the Israeli Army, the most highly trained of these units being 'Sayaret Matkal'. Matkal roughly translates as GHQ and indicates the unit's assignment directly to the Chief of Intelligence. This unit is Israel's deep penetration raiding force and counter-terrorist unit. It is drawn heavily from airborne personnel.

Also considered élite within the Israeli Army is the Golani Brigade, which though armoured infantry, often functions in a role akin to the US Rangers.

Combat swimmers of the Israeli navy can carry out underwater infiltration and other typical frogman missions.

Israeli airborne training includes a rigorous selection course, but jump school lasts only three weeks during which men make five jumps – three day and two night. Women undergo a two-week course during which they make three day jumps. To be designated an advanced parachutist requires fifty jumps. An instructor-jump-master has to complete the six months' instructor course and have made at least sixty jumps. Upon completing this course, an instructor is eligible for the free-fall rating after making at least ten free-fall jumps.

Israeli paras wear a red beret and members of the Golani Brigade wear a brown beret. Another noteworthy distinction is the coloured plastic background to the parachute badge. White designates an instructor, red a combat jump, green a Commando, blue basic para status, and black formerly meant a water jump or 'Armour Commando'. As of 1983, graduates of the airborne school assigned to any infantry unit wear the green background as do airborne-qualified Commandos. Parachute-qualified troops assigned to other branches still wear the wings on the blue background. Anyone with a double qualification may wear more than one colour backing overlapping.

PLATE 35: ISRAEL

11 Airborne Central Command arm shield
12 Unidentified
13 Airborne Maintenance
14 Airborne Brigade
15 Airborne Commando (Southern Command)
16 Unidentified
17 Airborne Brigade Reserve
18 Airborne School (Special) (i.e., snipers, etc.)
19 Airborne Infantry School
20 29th Parachute Brigade
21 Unidentified
22 Airborne Artillery
23 Unidentified
24 Airborne Brigade Reserve
25 Airborne Unit Reserve
26 Airborne Division Reserve
27 Unidentified
28 13th Parachute Brigade

PLATE 35

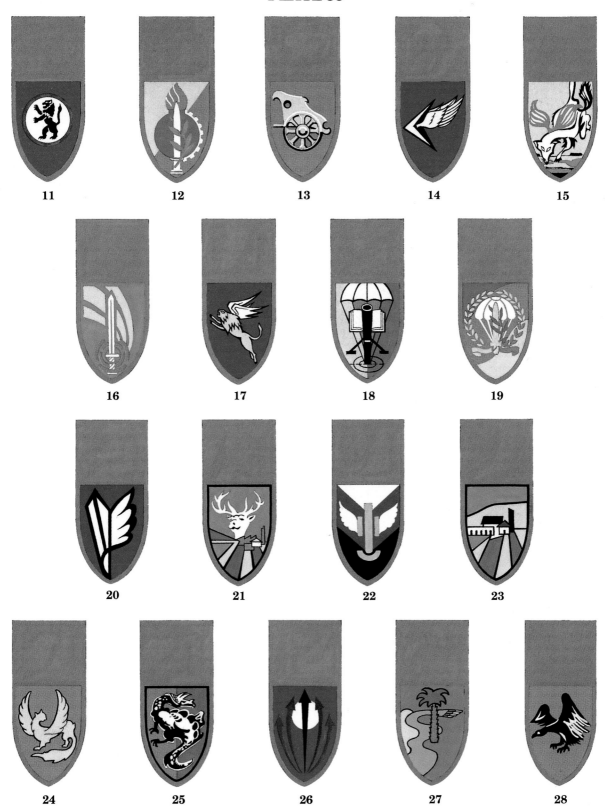

11

12

13

14

15

16

17

18

19

20

21

22

23

24

25

26

27

28

PLATE 36: SYRIA

Syria's first parachute unit was formed in 1958 and by the 1970s had increased to three battalions. Additionally, there are eight Commando battalions organized into two brigades. The Presidential Guard Unit is trained for the special forces mission as well. During the Yom Kippur War, Syrian Commandos particularly won the admiration of Israel's Golani Brigade and the paratroopers who had to dislodge them from positions on the Golan Heights. Men of the 82nd Parachute Battalion took part in this fighting as well. Once again, during the Israeli invasion of Lebanon in 1982, Syrian Commandos proved their toughest opposition.

The Syrians refer to their Commando battalions as 'Fugs'; they are comprised of three highly trained companies of airmobile élite infantry. The Syrians seem to make it a point to commit their Commandos to combat as frequently as possible thus reinforcing their training and *esprit de corps* with combat experience.

1 1st Commando Battalion badge; note the 1st Battalion uses a black shield; each of the other seven battalions uses a different colour
2 Commando Battalion badge
3 Commando Battalion badge
4 Variation of Nos. 1–3
5 Variation of Nos. 1–3
6 Insignia of one of the two Commando Brigades
7 Commando Brigade insignia; the purpose of the black bar is not known
8 Airborne Brigade patch
9 Commando Brigade insignia

▲Syrian paratrooper wearing the very colourful, late-style parachutist's brevet. (Adrian Bohlen)

PLATE 36 CONTINUED: MOROCCO

Morocco has a parachute brigade, members of which have seen action when on detachment with the Syrians against Israel and on detachment in Zaire. Others fought against insurgents in the Spanish Sahara. The brigade is based near Rabat International Airport at the same installation where the Moroccan parachute school is located. Parachute troops wear the same green beret worn by other members of the Army.

Within its Gendarmerie, Morocco also has a counter-terrorist unit bearing the same initials (GIGN) as the French counter-terrorist unit.
1 Airborne collar insignia
2 Airborne pocket badge (normally with green background rather than grey)
3 Variation of No. 2

PLATE 36 CONTINUED: SUDAN

Sudan's airborne forces were founded in 1962 when a group of instructors was trained in Great Britain, but the Sudanese Parachute Battalion was not formed until 1964. Currently, the Sudan has an 'Airborne Corps' based with the Parachute Training Centre at Khartoum. There is also an airborne Ranger unit as well. The basic airborne course consists of one month's physical training (to some extent based on the British P Company), then three weeks of ground and jump training including six jumps – three day, one day with deployment of the reserve chute, one day with equipment, and one night jump. Also receiving airborne training is the 144th Counter Terrorist Unit, one of the better such units in Africa. Airborne personnel wear a maroon beret.
1 Airborne officers' beret badge
2 Airborne shoulder tab
3 Airborne other ranks' beret badge
4 Airborne shoulder insignia

PLATE 36 CONTINUED: AFGHANISTAN

Afghanistan had an entire Special Forces Brigade – the 444th Commando Brigade – which was airborne qualified; however, through desertions and combat losses, this unit's strength may have fallen to battalion or less during the fighting against the Mujahadeen. At one point there was also a separate airborne battalion.
5 Airborne battalion shoulder insignia
6 444th Commando Brigade shoulder insignia

PLATE 36

PLATE 36 CONTINUED: IRAQ

During the 1960s Iraq formed a Special Forces Brigade with parachute and Commando troops. Members of this brigade saw action against the Israelis in the Yom Kippur War. Reportedly, too, many operations against the Iranians were carried out by Iraqi special forces during the Iran-Iraq War.

1 Airborne beret or collar insignia
2 Airborne shoulder insignia, worn on both shoulders
3 Special Forces Brigade insignia
4 Parachute School insignia

PLATE 36 CONTINUED: ALGERIA

Although Algeria had colonial parachute troops under the French, it was not until shortly after achieving independence in 1962 that Algerian Parachute Commando Battalions were formed under Soviet instruction.

1 Parachute Commando breast badge
2 Variation of No. 1

PLATE 36 CONTINUED: LEBANON

The disintegration of the Lebanese armed forces during the civil war created instability which did not lend itself well to the creation of special operations troops; however, there have been various élite units during the past two decades. Among Christian forces, the Guardians of the Cedar were an élite. Other units formed with US Special Forces advisers have included the Tactical Strike Unit and the Moukafaha, a special ops/counter-terrorist unit.

1 Gardiens du Cedre insignia
2 Obsolete Moukafaha shoulder title
3 Tactical Strike Force insignia (Bearing legend 'Strike Force' in Arabic)
4 Moukafaha insignia

▼Syrian Commandos wearing Commando pocket crests and parachute brevets of the type worn in Syria, Egypt and Libya with only slight differences. (Adrian Bohlen)

►Iraqi Commando in camouflage utilities.

▼Algerian paratrooper wears instructor's brevet and airborne collar insignia. (Adrian Bohlen)

▼Moroccan paratrooper wearing parachute instructor's brevet with airborne collar insignia and pocket crest. (Adrian Bohlen)

EUROPE

PLATE 37: BELGIUM

The current Belgian Airborne Commando Regiment evolved from those Belgian veterans of the British Commandos, SAS, and paras who formed the basis of the post-war Belgian airborne forces. Currently the Regiment is composed of three battalions, the 1st and 3rd of which wear the red beret of the paras and the 2nd the green beret of the Commandos. Initially, there had been separate parachute and Commando regiments, but they were merged in 1954. As a result all members of the regiment received training at the Belgian Commando School at Marche-les-Dames and at the Parachute School at Schaffen. During the later

1950s, the Para Commando Regiment increased dramatically in size as battalions and independent companies were sent to help maintain control of colonies in Africa, particularly the Congo. As Belgium withdrew from Africa in 1960, some of the battalions were disbanded. Members of the unit returned to the Congo in 1964, however, to rescue European civilians during the civil war. In May 1978, the 1st and 3rd Battalions of the Para Commando Regiment were air lifted to Kolwezi, Zaire, to follow up the combat jump by the French 2nd Régiment Etrangère Parachutiste.

The current organization of the regiment includes the three airborne/Commando infantry battalions plus

1 Obsolete 3rd Para Battalion beret badge
2 UDA (Air base defence unit) beret badge
3 Para Regiment beret badge
4 1st Para Battalion beret badge
5 2nd Commando Battalion beret badge
6 Para artillery beret badge
7 181st Quartermaster Company (aerial delivery) beret badge; note, on Belgian beret badges normally gold indicates an officer, silver an NCO and bronze, other ranks
8 Para collar insignia
9 Commando collar insignia
10 Anti-tank company distinctive insignia
11 Plastic insignia for para/Commando combat swimmers
12 Metal-coloured insignia for para/Commando combat swimmers

13 Plastic insignia for para/Commando mountain leaders
14 Metal-coloured insignia for mountain leaders
15 Para/Commando anti-tank squadron crest
16 Unidentified
17 Airborne collar patch 1st and 3rd Para Battalions
18 Airborne shoulder slide 1st and 3rd Para Battalions
19 Obsolete 3rd Para Battalion collar insignia
20 Obsolete 3rd Para Battalion shoulder slide
21 Collar insignia for 181st Quartermaster Company (Aerial Delivery)
22 Shoulder loops for 181st QM Company
23 Commando collar patch
24 Commando shoulder slide
25 Commando shoulder arc

PLATE 37

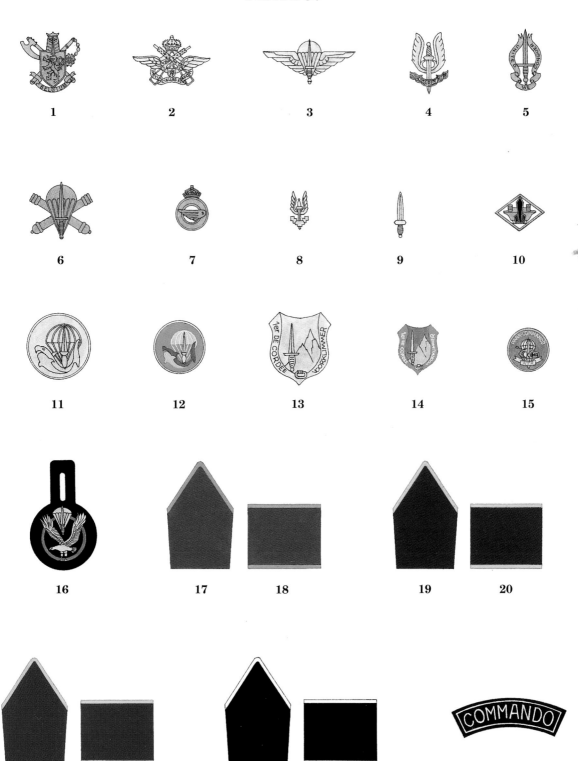

1

2

3

4

5

6

7

8

9

10

11

12

13

14

15

16

17

18

19

20

21

22

23

24

25

an HQ, parachute training school, Commando training school, anti-tank company, light armoured recon squadron, artillery battery, combat swimmer detachment and mountain leader detachment. Operating separately is the Equipes Spéciales de Reconnaissance (ESR) based at the International LRRP School in Germany and carrying out a similar mission to other NATO LRRP units.

Recruits undergo four months' training before receiving their Commando brevet, then one month's parachute training before receiving their parachute brevet. Interestingly, from 1976 women have been allowed to enlist in the regiment and some have completed both Commando and parachute training, though they were normally assigned to administrative jobs within the regiment. Those graduating from the full para-Commando course wear the 'A' brevet, achieved after making eight jumps, three from a balloon, five from an aircraft, including one equipment and one night jump. Other Army personnel not assigned to the Para Commandos have often completed the shorter 2-week course for the 'B' brevet in which they make five jumps, four balloon and one aircraft. There is also a dispatcher/jumpmaster brevet for those who are career officers or NCOs, who hold an 'A' brevet, have served two years with an airborne unit, and have completed a 6-month instructor's course which includes free-fall training.

PLATE 38: BELGIUM

26 Commando shoulder insignia
27 Commando Training Centre insignia
28 Para right sleeve insignia
29 Para left sleeve insignia
30 Combat swimmer insignia
31 Para/Commando Regiment blazer patch
32 2nd Commando Battalion blazer patch
33 1st Para Battalion blazer patch
34 3rd Para Battalion blazer patch
35 3rd Para Battalion sports patch
36 3rd Para Battalion shoulder patch
37 Air Commando shoulder arc
38 Kamina Air Base, the Congo, shoulder flash
39 Airborne School patch
40 Combat swimmer pocket patch
41 Anti-tank squadron blazer patch
42 Para/Commando Medical Centre blazer patch
43 Para/Commando Recce Squadron blazer patch
44 Para/Commando Training Centre blazer patch
45 USN (?) Commando blazer patch
46 Para/Commando artillery blazer patch
47 Belgian Army parachute team sport patch

◀ *A typical combat scenario for the élite fighting man. This Belgian Special Forces soldier trains for the type of environment he may well have to fight in, here using the 5.56mm Minimi light machine-gun, which is well designed for operating in adverse conditions.*

PLATE 38

26

27

28

29

30

31

32

33

34

35

36

37

38

39

40

41

42

43

44

45

46

47

GREAT BRITAIN

Within the British Army the term 'élite' has been interpreted differently at different times. For example, traditionally, the Guards Regiments have comprised an 'élite'; however, within the context of this book only the no-longer extant Guards Independent Parachute Company would qualify as élite. Among those units that will be discussed are the Royal Marine Commandos, tracing as they do their heritage to the Second World War Commandos, the first of Great Britain's special forces units. Currently the Commando Brigade consists of three 'Commandos' – Numbers 40, 42 and 45. Each of these Commadnos has a strength of 680 officers and men. Support for the Commandos comes from Commando-trained Royal Marine support troops and Commando-trained members of the Army in the Commando Logistic Regiment, 29 Commando Regiment, Royal Artillery, and 59 Independent Commando Squadron, Royal Engineers. In addition to having undergone the rigorous Commando Training Course, a substantial percentage of Commandos are also parachute, ski, mountain, and scuba trained. In fact, at least 10 per cent of all Royal Marines are parachute-trained and more than 50 per cent are ski-trained. Two élite-within-an-élite specialist units are the Mountain and Arctic Warfare cadre and the Special Boat Squadron, the latter being the equivalent of the US SEALs or Marine Recons. There is also a specialist company – Comacchio Company – trained for anti-terrorist duties, protecting the North sea oil-fields. Additionally, there are approximately 1,500 Royal Marine reservists.

Within the Army are two élite units: the Special Air Service and the Parachute Regiment. The Special Air Service (SAS) consists of one regular regiment – 22nd SAS Regiment, and two Reserve (Territorial Army) regiments – 21st and 23rd SAS. Trained to carry out deep penetration scouting and raids, anti-terrorist operations, counter-insurgency and various other special operations, the SAS Regiment is broken down into squadrons, each of about 64 men. Each squadron is further broken down into four 16-man troops, each specializing in amphibious/boat, mountain/arctic, mobility, or air-parachute skills. The selection course for the SAS is very rigorous and is designed to select those with the necessary combination of intelligence, initiative, stamina, and discipline.

The Parachute Regiment is the élite parachute light infantry formation of the British Army and is comprised of three battalions, all of which are fully parachute-trained, though prior to the Falklands War only one battalion would normally have been on jump status at a time. In 1984, however, 5th Infantry Brigade was re-designated 5th Airborne Brigade with more of the parachute infantryman on jump status as well as parachute-trained elements of the Royal Engineers, Royal Artillery, and other support and service arms assigned. Additionally, there are three reserve (TA) battalions and one reserve independent parachute company as follows: 4th Battalion drawn from the North Midlands and the north-east, 10th Battalion drawn from London, 15th Battalion drawn from Scotland, and the 16th Independent Parachute Company drawn from Lincoln.

The Royal Air Force maintains its own light infantry regiment – the RAF Regiment – for base defence, though it has also traditionally been used on counter-insurgency and other light infantry missions. No 2

PLATE 39: BRITISH

1 Bright version of the Parachute Regiment cap badge adopted in 1943; until 1952 it was worn in the King's Crown version and since then in the Queen's Crown style as illustrated
2 'Subdued' (non-reflective) version of the Parachute Regiment cap badge
3 Parachute Regiment collar insignia in the same style as the regimental cap badge
4 & 5 Parachute Regiment buttons as worn on the No. 1 dress uniform
6 Parachute Regiment right shoulder insignia
7 Parachute Regiment left shoulder insignia
8 Parachute Regiment stable belt
9 Special Air Service wire cap badge; note the silver/gold wire; although traditionally called the 'winged dagger', this badge was initially intended to represent a winged Excalibur

10 Special Air Service other ranks' cap badge; note the embroidery
11 SAS collar insignia worn with the Nos. 1 and 2 dress uniforms
12 Variation of No. 11 which is slightly smaller
13 Special Air Service shoulder arc
14 Crossbelt 'Mars and Minerva' badge worn by members of 21 Special Air Service Regiment
15 The 'Mars and Minerva' cap badge of the Artists Rifles worn by members of 21st SAS during 1948–9, but then replaced by the standard winged dagger cap badge
16 Shoulder-strap rank slide in the rank of staff sergeant, but also available in other ranks and worn on the 'woolly pully' sweater
17 Shoulder-strap rank slide on DPM material, reportedly worn by members of 21st and 23rd SAS but possibly a 'fantasy' item created for collectors
18 Special Air Service stable belt

PLATE 39

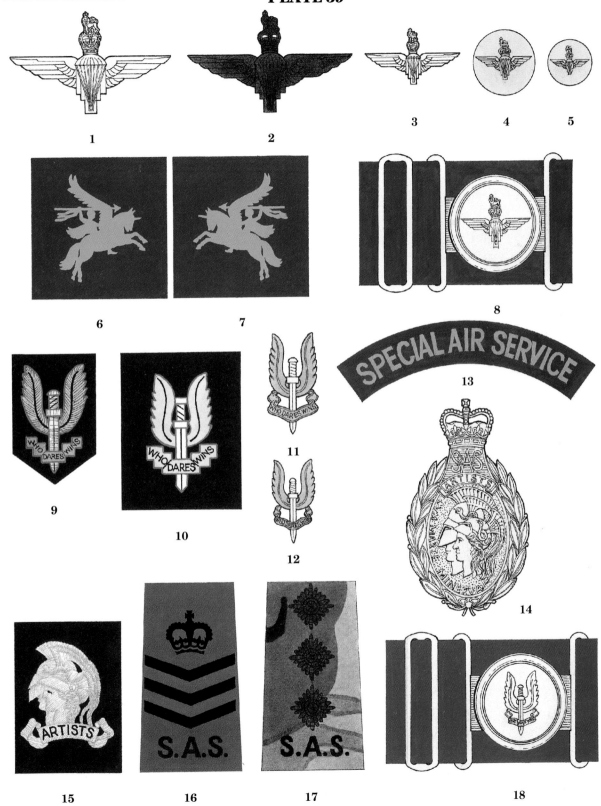

1

2

3

4

5

6

7

8

9

10

11

12

SPECIAL AIR SERVICE

13

14

15

16

17

18

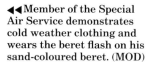◄◄Member of the Special Air Service demonstrates cold weather clothing and wears the beret flash on his sand-coloured beret. (MOD)

◄Member of the SAS in Malaya wears the beret flash on the maroon beret that was worn at that time, and the SAS wings on the shoulder. (MOD)

▼Royal Marine engineer in the Falklands helps remove mines sown during the conflict. Note that he

wears the Royal Marines Commando shoulder arc with parachute wings. A substantial percentage of

the Royal Marines are parachute-qualified. (Imperial War Museum)
▼Royal Marine in the

Falklands War offers a good view of the Commando beret badge. (Imperial War Museum)

▶Prince Charles as Colonel in Chief of the Parachute Regiment wears the Regimental beret badge on his maroon beret. (Imperial War Museum)

Squadron of the RAF Regiment is parachute-trained and is considered the élite squadron of the RAF Regiment, capable of carrying out parachute assaults or other types of special missions.

As with many other armed forces, those of Great Britain use berets to identify élite troops. The Royal Marine Commandos wear their traditional green beret; they, in fact, established the green beret as a symbol of military élite status; while the SAS wears a sand-coloured beret, the Parachute Regiment a red beret; which gives them their title the 'Red Devils'; and the RAF Regiment a blue beret.

PLATE 40: BRITISH ROYAL MARINES, CANADA, NEW ZEALAND, AUSTRALIA

19 Royal Marines bright beret/cap badge; all gilt as shown is for other ranks, while officers and Warrant Officers I have a silver globe and gilt laurels
20 Royal Marines subdued beret/cap badge
21 Royal Marines shoulder arc
22 Members of various regiments attend the Commando qualification course and are authorized to wear a small qualification badge bearing the traditional commando dagger signifying completion. This badge – gold on green – is for the Highland regiments
23 Commando qualification – gold on black – Royal Electrical and Mechanical Engineers
24 As above – gold on red – line infantry
25 As above – gold on maroon – Parachute Regiment
26 As above – silver on red – Lowland Scots Regiments
27 As above – silver on black – Royal Tank Corps
28 Specialist qualification badge for a swimmer-canoeist 3rd Class; Royal Marine qualification badges are gold on blue for ceremonial, blue and gold on green for Lovat dress
29 Swimmer canoeist 2nd Class
30 Swimmer canoeist 1st Class
31 An unathorized badge made as a novelty for members of the Special Boat Squadron, with a frog with oars and the Royal Marines' red parachute wings; the disc-shaped insignia bears the SBS motto 'Not by Strength. By Guile'
32 Mountain leader 1st Class
33 Mountain leader 2nd Class
34 First-pattern Drop Zone flash for No. 2 Squadron, RAF Regiment
35 Second-pattern Drop Zone flash for No. 2 Squadron, RAF Regiment, adopted in June 1978

CANADA

Canadian airborne capability was directed against the perceived threat of Soviet airborne landings and an airborne/air transportable formation, the Mobile Striking Force, was formed based on three infantry battalions, an artillery battery and support units. In 1958, as the Soviet threat diminished the Mobile Striking Force became a single battalion known as The Defence of Canada Force.

In April 1968 airborne elements of the Canadian armed forces were concentrated into the Canadian Airborne Regiment and, with a strength of 900 troops, was a rapidly deployable force for use in Canada or abroad. Two airborne Commandos and an artillery battery provided the primary combat elements supported by airborne engineers and other troops.

The Canadian airborne forces relocated to Petawawa, Ontario in July 1977, forming the basis of the

Special Service Force, the current Canadian airborne unit. From 1979 the Airborne Regiment gained a third Commando, giving it three Commandos of 154 men each. While elements of the regiment are parachute-qualified, most of the Special Service Force is air-transportable rather than airborne. Since the US Special Forces and the Special Service Force trace their lineage to the 1st Special Service Force of the Second World War, members of the Special Service Force have traditionally attended the Special Forces selection course at Fort Bragg, and the six-week Patrol Pathfinder Course combines some elements of the US Ranger training with Pathfinder training.

1 Version of the Special Service Force formation sign worn on the service dress uniform; OSONS stands for 'Let Us Dare'

2 Version of the SSF formation sign worn on the jump smock and combat dress

3 A prototype shoulder title proposed in 1977, but which was not adopted; however, most of the titles were sold to members of the Airborne Regiment as souvenirs

NEW ZEALAND

Despite approval for the formation of a New Zealand SAS Squadron to operate with the British 22nd SAS in Malaya in 1954, selection and training delayed availability for action to 1955. Arriving in November and December 1955, the squadron underwent parachute training at Singapore and jungle training at Perak, and after spending 24 months in Malaya, the squadron returned to New Zealand in 1957 and disbanded.

In December 1959 a single troop was re-activated and until 1965 parachute training took place in Australia, continuing thereafter at Wheupai. In 1962 a New Zealand SAS detachment was deployed to Thailand to work with US Army Special Forces and US Marines, performing reconnaissance missions and training the Thais. A second detachment was sent to fight alongside the British SAS in Borneo in 1964, followed by three others over the following two years. In November 1968 No. 4 Troop of the New Zealand SAS was sent to Vietnam, serving as part of an Australian SAS squadron and remaining in Vietnam until February 1971.

Today the New Zealand SAS group, based at Papakura Military Base near Auckland, follows a parachute course requiring eight jumps, including two equipment jumps and one night jump.

An interesting uniform note is that until 1986 the New Zealand SAS had maroon berets but now wear the same sand-coloured beret as the British and Australian SAS.

4 Shoulder arc worn by members of the New Zealand Special Air Service

AUSTRALIA

The primary special forces unit in the Australian armed forces is the Australian Special Air Service Regiment, formed in July 1957. Initially independent for three years as 1st SAS Company, the unit was then incorporated into the Royal Australian Regiment. However, the Borneo Confrontation and the need for larger special forces capability led to the 1st SAS Company being expanded to two squadrons, forming the Australian Special Air Service Regiment in September 1964. After intensive training both squadrons saw service in the counter-insurgency and cross-border roles from February 1965 to August 1966.

In 1962 members of the Australian SAS became part of the Australian Army Training Team – Vietnam and the 3rd Squadron was sent to Vietnam in July 1966. Until 1971 each squadron did two tours in Vietnam, establishing a reputation for tough professionalism and as experts at long-range patrolling. Since Vietnam the Australian SAS has been active in reconnaissance, amphibious, anti-terrorist, and special operations roles.

As in all SAS units, selection and training is rigorous and the Australian SAS initial selection course includes a timed navigational exercise over rough terrain. Having passed the initial stage, the candidate undertakes a five-week familiarization course, a four-week long-range patrol course and a three-week parachute course at Nowra, New South Wales. Training continues to stress specialized skills. Completion of all training brings the sand-coloured beret bearing the SAS beret badge, although Australians wear a metal beret badge on the cloth background rather than the British cloth beret badge.

Companion to the SAS, the Royal Australian Regiment is also airborne-qualified. The three-week basic course was only twelve actual training days in 1987 during which the trainee made nine jumps. SAS members and instructors also take a free-fall course making thirty to fifty descents after three days' training. There is also a small number of trained clearance divers in the Australian Navy: No. 1 Clearance Diver Team at Perth and No. 2 Clearance Diver Team at Sydney, operating akin to US SEAL/UDT teams. Finally the 1st Commando Regiment formed in 1980 gives a greater amphibious capability; peviously only reserve Commando formations with widespread Vietnam experience existed.

5 Commando beret badge

PLATE 40

19   20   21   22   23   24

25   26   27   28   29   30

31   32   33   34   35

1

2

NEW ZEALAND
SPECIAL AIR SERVICE

4

AIRBORNE AÉROPORTÉ
CANADA

3

5

PLATE 41: FRANCE

France's airborne forces have a rich and proud tradition dating back to before the Second World War. It was in Indo China (where French troops made more than 100 combat jumps) and Algeria that the para legend was forged. To understand French parachute units, one must appreciate the difference between the Colonial Paratroops (now the RPIMa), the Metro Paratroops, and the Legion Paratroops. The old Colonial Paratroops, who are now known as the Marine Paratroops (not because of any amphibious mission but because they are deployed on foreign service), were and are professionals who join with the understanding that they may be deployed outside France. The Metro paras were and are those who would normally only be deployed abroad in the event of full-scale hostilities. The Foreign Legion paras are professionals who may be deployed anywhere France deems necessary and who act as the principal rapid deployment element.

The principal French airborne unit today is the 11th Division Parachutiste based at Tarbes. Principal operational units within the 11th DP are seven parachute battalions: the 1st RPIMa, 3rd RPIMa, 6th RPIMA, and 8th RPIMa, 1st RCP (Régiment Chasseurs Parachutistes), 9th RCP, and 2nd REP (Régiment Etrangère Parachutiste). Artillery, engineer, signals, transport, logistical, and aviation units are also assigned. Independent of the 11th DP are the 2nd RPIMa and the 13th RDP (Régiment Dragons Parachutistes). Note that this latter unit functions as a long-range patrol, deep penetration raiding unit. The most recent French combat jump was in 1978 at Kolwezi, Zaire, where the 2nd REP jumped to rescue civilians under attack by rebels.

Prior to the creation of the 11th DP, there was a 25th Parachute Division, created in Algeria in 1956 and disbanded in 1961 after the putsch.

Among other units receiving parachute training are the Squadron Fusiliers Commandos Intervention of the Air Force; numerous members of the Marine Commandos, Naval Combat Swimmers, and members of the Gendarmarie Parachute unit as well as members of GIGN, the national counter-terrorist unit.

Legion paras wear a green beret; others wear the red beret – the famous beret 'rouge'. Air Force Commandos wear a black beret and Marine Commandos wear a green beret.

1 From 1946 to 1958 the Metro para beret badge; now the Legion para beret badge
2 First-type Colonial para beret badge, then the RPIMa beret badge
3 From 1962 to 1974 RPIMa beret badge
4 25th Brigade Aéroportée crest
5 1st Brigade Parachutiste crest
6 2nd Brigade Parachutiste crest
7 Etat-Major, 11th Division Parachutiste
8 11th DP/44th Division Militaire
9 Second type of No. 8
10 Etat-Major du Groupement Aéroportée
11 Détachement Barracuda
12 Variant of No. 1
13 French assistance elements Operation 'Bouar'
14 Crest for later designation for 'Barracuda' in the Central African Republic – Eléments Français d'Assistance d'Opérations
15 1st Régiment Chasseurs Parachutistes
16 Another version of the 1st RCP crest locally made in Indo-China
17 14th RCP
18 18th RCP
19 9th RCP
20 3rd Company of the 1st RCP
21 Compagnie d'Appui, 1st RCP
22 2nd Company of the 1st RCP
23 Compagnie d'Eclairage et d'Appui du 9th RCP

PLATE 41

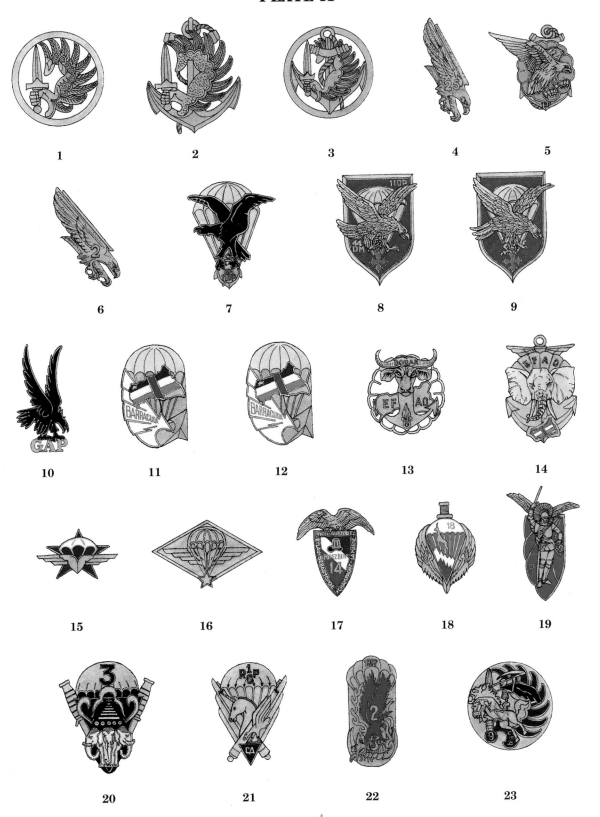

1

2

3

4

5

6

7

8

9

10

11

12

13

14

15

16

17

18

19

20

21

22

23

PLATE 42: FRANCE

24 11th Company of the 9th RCP
25 3rd Company of the RCP (apparently struck for a reunion)
26 Compagnie du Commandement et de Soutien du 9th RCP
27 1st Company of the 9th RCP
28 12th Company of the 9th RCP
29 Compagnie de Base du 9th RCP
30 2nd Compagnie du 9th RCP
31 SER of the 9th RCP
32 1st Company of the 1st RCP
33 4th Company of the 1st RCP
34 Groupement d'Instruction du 9th RCP
35 3rd Company of the 9th RCP
36 Détachement d'Assistance Operationelle du 1st RCP
37 12th Company of the 1st RCP
38 Variant of 37
39 Musicians of the 11th DP
40 Compagnie de Commandement et de Soutien du 1st RCP
41 3rd RCP
42 4th Company of the 9th RCP
43 Section Milan of the 9th RCP
44 11th Bataillon Parachutiste de Choc (shock or assault parachute battalion)
45 12th Bataillon Parachutiste de Choc
46 1st Bataillon Parachutiste de Choc

▼Members of France's élite counter-terrorist unit GIGN; note the shoulder sleeve insignia and the parachute brevet. (ECP)

PLATE 42

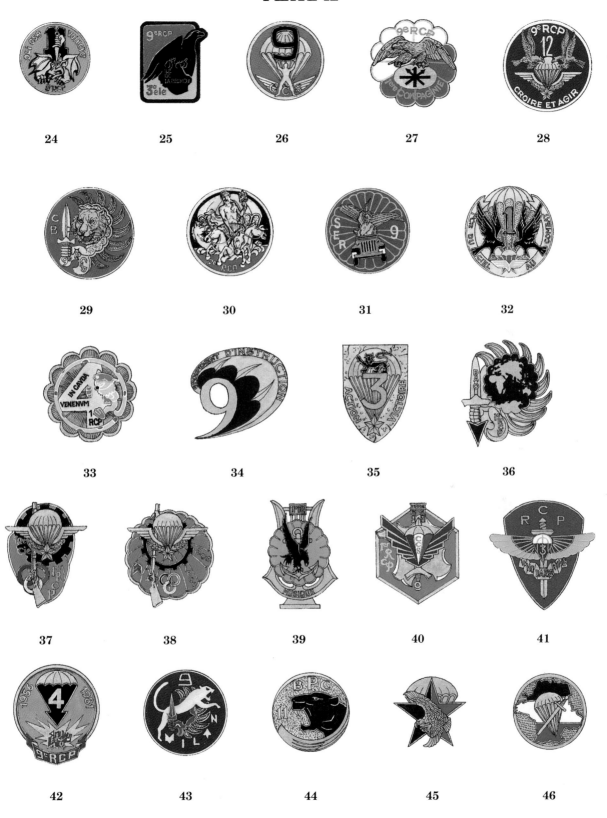

24

25

26

27

28

29

30

31

32

33

34

35

36

37

38

39

40

41

42

43

44

45

46

PLATE 43: LEGION PARATROOP INSIGNIA

1 Parachute Company of the 3rd REI Pocket Crest (note this was the original Legion para unit)
2 1st Foreign Legion Para Battalion
3 1st Foreign Legion Para Regiment (the famous 1st REP disbanded in Algeria after the attempted putsch)
4 2nd Foreign Legion Para Battalion, later Regiment
5 Compagnie Etrangère de Revitaillement par Air (one of the rarest and most sought after of all French insignia, sometimes fetching prices in excess of $2,000)
6 3rd Foreign Legion Para Regiment
7 1st Foreign Legion Para Heavy Mortar Company
8 3rd Company, 2nd REP
9 2nd Company, 2nd REP (first type)
10 4th Company, 2nd REP
11 2nd Company, 2nd REP (second type)

12 1st Company, 2nd REP
Note: Items 13–17 were produced in the USA and were never officially adopted by the 2nd REP though they may have been worn by some unit members unofficially
13 Amphibious Company of the 2nd REP (each of the four parachute infantry companies has a speciality; the 3rd Cie is amphibious/small boat)
14 2nd Company, 2nd REP (mountain/ski specialists)
15 Recon and Tactical Support Company, 2nd REP (includes LRRP and HALO personnel)
16 Administrative and Logistical Support Company, 2nd REP
17 HALO teams (free-fall parachutists), 2nd REP

▼Members of the 2nd French Foreign Legion Parachute Regiment offer a good view of the legion parachute beret badge. Note also the tailored uniforms so common in the Legion.

PLATE 43

1   2   3   4

5   6   7   8

9   10   11   12   13

14   15   16   17

PLATE 44: COLONIAL PARAS AND RPIMA

1 2nd RPC (Régiment Colonial Parachutiste)/RPIMa: note the SAS wing harking back to the Second World War French SAS
2 3rd RPIMa
3 6th RPIMa
4 7th RPIMa
5 8th RPIMa
6 Compagnie Parachutiste d'Infanterie de Marine
7 5th Battalion RPIMa
8 8th RPIMa (Type 2)
9 1st RPIMa
10 1st Régiment Inter-Armes d'Outre-Mer
11 Section Entac du 8th RPIMa
12 Section d'Eclairage Régimentaire du 8th RPIMa
13 Section de Saut Operationnale Grande Hauteur du 8th RPIMa
14 3rd RPIMa in Chad
15 Milan Section 6th RPIMa
16 Compagnie d'Eclairage et d'Appui 8th RPIMa
17 Section de Saut Operationnale Grande Hauteur du 3rd RPIMa
18 1st RPIMa musicians
19 11th Company, 6th RPIMa
20 Transmissions, 6th RPIMa
21 3rd Company, 6th RPIMa
22 3nd Company, 6th RPIMa

▼Members of France's GIGN wear the parachute brevet on the right breast, while the man on the left wears the Commando brevet on the left breast. (ECP

PLATE 44

1

2

3

4

5

6

7

8

9

10

11

12

13

14

15

16

17

18

19

20

21

22

PLATE 45: FRANCE

1 1st Régiment de Hussards Parachutistes
2 13th Régiment de Dragons Parachutistes
3 Peloton Kieger (Type I)
4 Anti-tank Platoon, 1st Squadron, 1st RHP (Type I)
5 4th Recon Platoon, 3rd Squadron, 1st RHP
6 Anti-tank Platoon, 4th Squadron, 1st RHP
7 HQ & Service Squadron, 1st RHP
8 Variant of No. 7
9 Peloton Kieger (Type II)
10 1st Squadron, 1st RHP Chad
11 Section de la Fanfare, 1st RHP
12 Anti-tank platoon, 10th RH
13 1st Squadron, 1st RHP in the Central African
Republic

14 Peloton Kieger in the Ivory Coast
15–23 Note these items are American-made and in
most cases havenot been officially adopted though
they may have been considered and even worn within
the units
15 Anti-tank Platoon, 1st Squadron, 1st RHP
16 4th Platoon, 4th Squadron, 1st RHP
17 1st Platoon, 4th Squadron, 1st RHP
18 2nd Anti-tank Platoon, 3rd Squadron, 1st RHP
19 Anti-tank Platoon, 1st Squadron, 1st RHP
20 2nd Platoon, 2nd Squadron, 1st RHP
21 1st Platoon, 4th Squadron, 1st RHP
22 Anti-tank Platoon, 4th Squadron, 1st RHP
23 35th Parachute Artillery Regiment

◀ *A fine detailed study of a
paratrooper of the 3rd
RPIMa (Régiment
Parachutiste d'Infanterie
de Marine) in New
Caledonia, 1985.*

PLATE 45

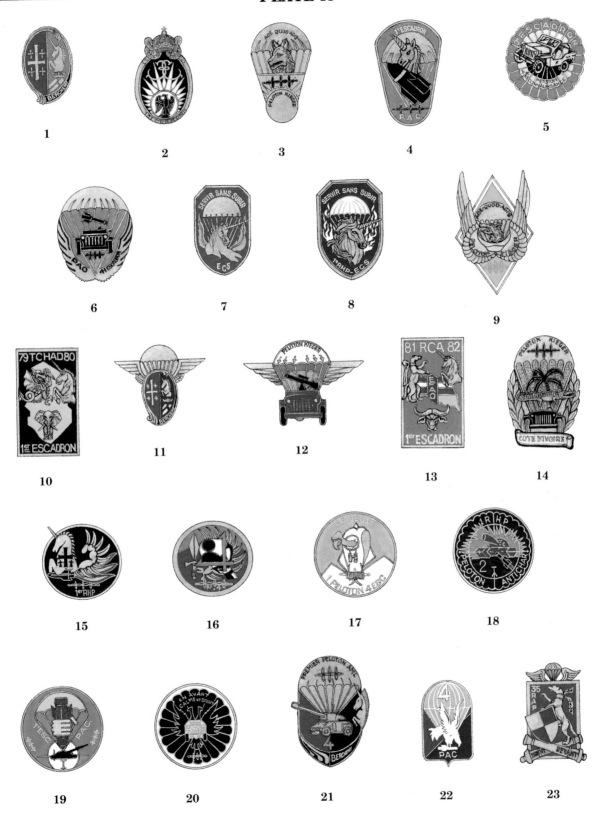

1

2

3

4

5

6

7

8

9

10

11

12

13

14

15

16

17

18

19

20

21

22

23

PLATE 46: FRANCE

24 20th Parachute Artillery Group
25 3rd Battery, 35th Parachute Artillery Regiment
25 3rd Battery, 35th Parachute Artillery Regiment
26 Training Battery, 35th Parachute Artillery Regiment
27 20mm AA, 35th Parachute Artillery Regiment
28 1st Battery, 35th Parachute Artillery Regiment
29 Aviation Platoon, 10th Parachute Division
30 Variant of No. 29
31 Mixed Aviation Platoon, 25th Parachute Division
32 Mixed Aviation Platoon, 11th Division
33 Etablissement de Réserve Générale du Matériel Alat et Aéroportée

34 5th Combat Helicopter Regiment
35 5th Groupement de Soutien de l'Alat
36 5th Combat Helicopter Regiment (Type II)
37 17th Airborne Engineer Battalion
38 17th Airborne Engineer Battalion (Tpe II)
39 60th Airborne Engineer Company
40 75th (later 61st) Airborne Engineer Company
41 Engineer Group Chad, 17th Airborne Engineer Regiment
42 1st Company, 17th Parachute Engineer Regiment
43 60th Parachute Signals Company
44 61st Airborne Signals Battalion
45 61st Command and Signals Battalion
46 425th Compagnie Légère Transmissions (Signals)
47 1st Parachute Signals Company

◄ France places great emphasis on maintaining sniper capability its special forces. This one is training with the FR-F1 rifle at Nîmes in 1990.

PLATE 46

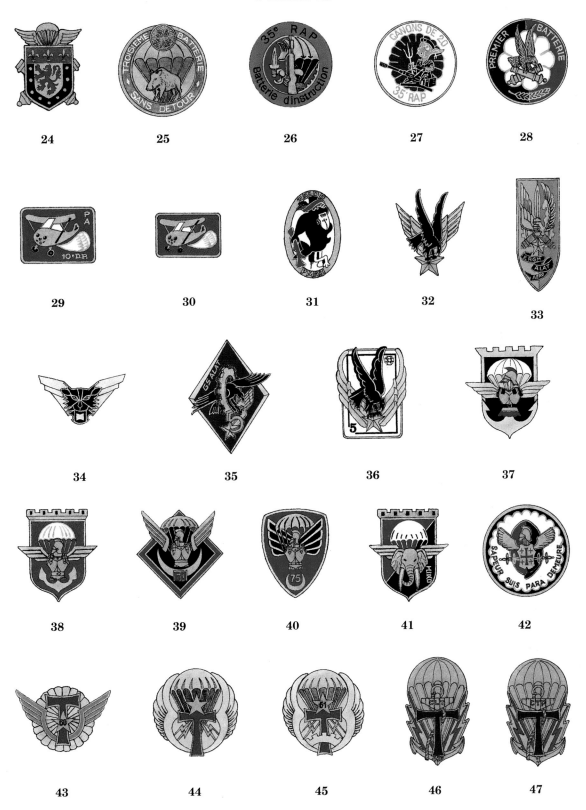

24

25

26

27

28

29

30

31

32

33

34

35

36

37

38

39

40

41

42

43

44

45

46

47

PLATE 47: FRANCE

48 Transport Group 513
49 75th HQ Company, Parachute Intervention Group
50 60th HQ Company, Parachute Intervention Group
51 Centre d'Instruction du Train 155
52 507th Transport Group
53 513th Transport Group
54 507th Transport Group (Type II)
55 61st HQ Company, 11th Division Légère d'Intervention
56 CIT 155 (Type II)

57 61st HQ Company, 11th Division
58 Groupe d'Escadron du Train 513
59 61st HQ Squadron, 11th Division
60 61st HQ Squadron, 11th Parachute Division
61 425th Transport and Traffic Squadron
62 1st Transport and Traffic Squadron, 1st BPCS
63 1st Air Delivery Company
64 2nd Air Delivery Company
65 3rd Air Delivery Company
66 4th Air Delivery Company, Troupes de Marine
67 Air Drop Squadron, 1st Air Delivery Company
68 Air Delivery Regiment

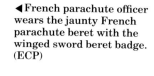

◀French parachute officer wears the jaunty French parachute beret with the winged sword beret badge. (ECP)

PLATE 47

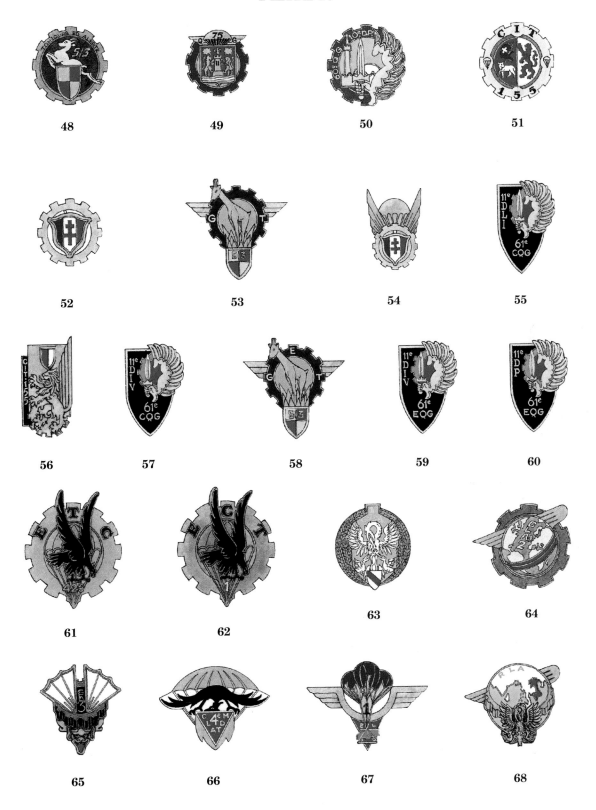

48

49

50

51

52

53

54

55

56

57

58

59

60

61

62

63

64

65

66

67

68

PLATE 48: FRANCE

◄*A paratrooper of the 2nd REP, camouflaged and ready to jump while training in Corsica.*

PLATE 48

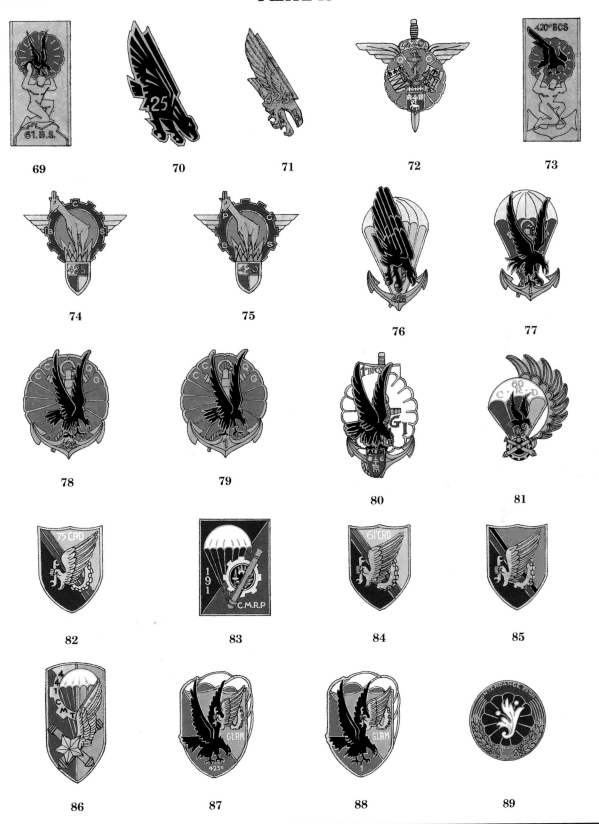

69

70

71

72

73

74

75

76

77

78

79

80

81

82

83

84

85

86

87

88

89

PLATE 49: FRANCE

▲*Legionnaires of the DLEM – the Détachement de Légion Etrangère – at Mayotte, well armed and spread out while training on an island in the Indian Ocean.*

PLATE 49

90

91

92

93

94

95

96

97

98

99

100

101

102

103

104

105

106

107

108

109

PLATE 50: FRANCE IN LEBANON

Note, most of the commemorative badges made for French airborne forces in Lebanon were in two versions – French-manufactured and locally-manufactured, the latter being much rougher in finish.

1 Beret insignia
2 Variant of No. 1
3 3rd RPIMa
4 Variant of No. 3
5 Signals, 3rd RPIMa
6 1st Company, 17th RGAP (Type I)
7 BOMAP (Type I)
8 Movement Control (Type I)
9 SMR 1
10 420th DSL
11 Combat Support Company, 420th DSL, 13th Mordat
12 420th Détachement de Soutien Logistique (DSL)
13 Military Police in Lebanon (Type I)
14 Régiment Français de l'Onu
15 Signals Section, 8th RPIMa
16 8th RPIMa (Type I)
17 3rd Company, 17th Parachute Engineer Regiment (Type I)
18 Transport Squadron, 420th DSL
19 1st Squadron, 1st RHP
20 Support Platoon, 1st RHP
21 Provisions Platoon, 420th DSL
22 Transport, 420th DSL
23 Movement Control (Type II)
24 Mobile Airborne Operating Base (BOMAP) (Type II)

▲ *A section of the 2ème REP in duty in Chad 1989.*

PLATE 50

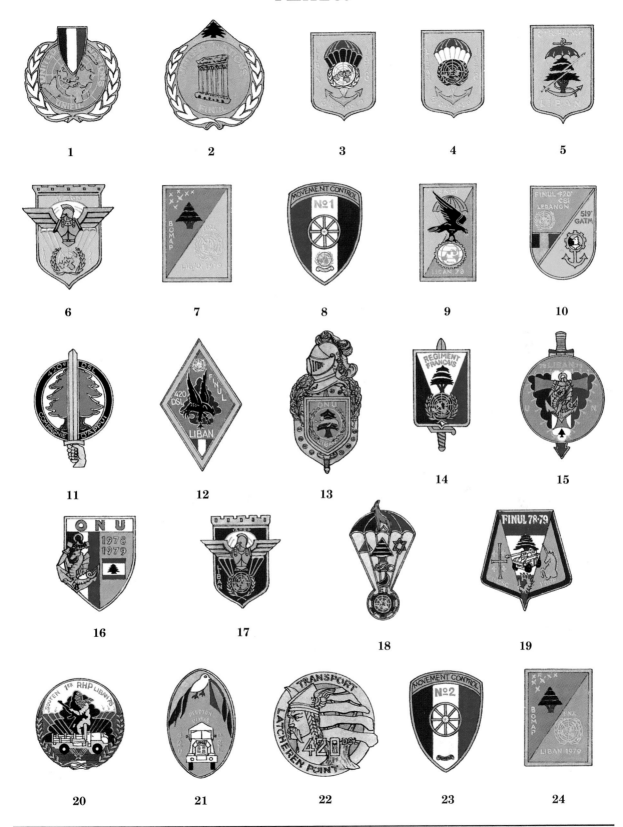

1

2

3

4

5

6

7

8

9

10

11

12

13

14

15

16

17

18

19

20

21

22

23

24

PLATE 51: FRANCE IN LEBANON

25 Détachement Santé du 420th DSL
26 420th Materials Company
27 Section d'Intervention du 425th DSL
28 Movement Control (Type III)
29 2nd Company, 17th Parachute Engineer Regiment
30 French Log – MP
31 425th DSL
32 3rd Company, 17th Parachute Engineer Regiment (Type II)
33 Compagnie d'Eclairage et d'Appui, 9th RCP
34 MP Company
35 Compagnie de Commandement, d'Organisation et des Services du 420th DSL (Type I)
36 2nd Company, 17th Parachute Engineer Regiment (Type II)
37 14th Parachute Command and Support Regiment
38 1st Company, 6th RPIMa
39 Section d'Intervention, 3rd Company, 1st RCP
40 1st RCP
41 9th RCP
42 French Log Battalion
43 Movement Company (Type IV)
44 2nd Company, 9th RCP
45 3rd Company, 6th RPIMa
46 Movement Control (Type V)
47 Compagnie d'Eclairage et d'Appui du 6th RPIMa

◀ *In parade dress, this is a legionnaire of the DLEM, the Détachement de lègion Etrangère, at Mayotte.*

PLATE 51

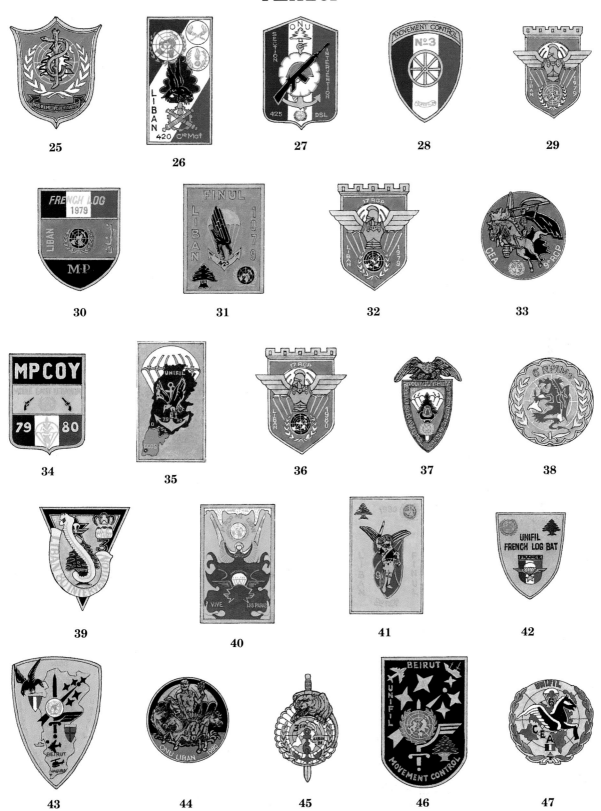

25

26

27

28

29

30

31

32

33

34

35

36

37

38

39

40

41

42

43

44

45

46

47

PLATE 52: FRANCE IN LEBANON

48 1st Company, 17th Parachute Engineer Regiment
49 Procurement Company, 420th DSL
50 Prévoté au Liban (Type II)
51 Section d'Intervention, 1st RCP
52 11th Company, 6th RPIMa
53 4th Squadron, 1st RHP
54 Support Company, 17th Parachute Engineer Regiment
55 1st Company, 9th RCP
56 3rd Company, 17th Parachute Engineer Regiment
57 Movement Control (Type VI)
58 Compagnie de Commandement d'Organisation et de Soutien du 420th DSL (Type II)
59 Movement Control (Type VII)
60 Section d'Intervention, 1st RHP
61 Compagnie de Commandement d'Organisation et de Soutien du 420th DSL (Type III)
62 8th RPIMa
63 2nd Company, 17th Parachute Engineer Regiment (Type III)
64 420th DSL (Type II)
65 Force Multinational d'Interposition Beyrauth
66 1st Company, 17th RGP/FMS
67 3rd RPIMa
68 8th RPIMa
69 1st RHP
70 17th RGP

◀ *Typical of the conditions in which today's élite units must fight: this French soldier with full pack, and his rifle at the ready, is fording a river. (Courtesy of Ian V. Hogg)*

PLATE 52

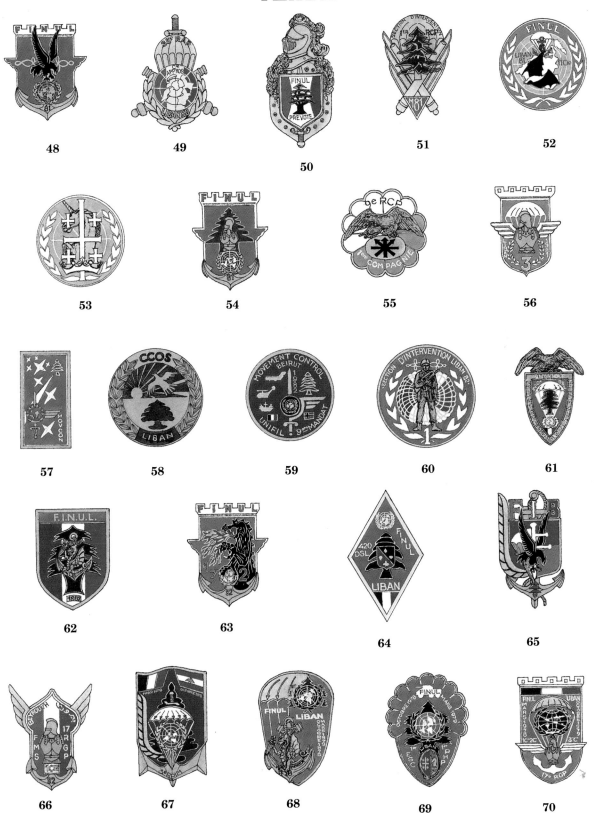

48

49

50

51

52

53

54

55

56

57

58

59

60

61

62

63

64

65

66

67

68

69

70

WEST GERMANY

Germany had been one of the pioneers of airborne troops during the years prior to the Second World War, and in 1956 as part of the re-establishment of the Federal Republic's armed forces, the 1st Airborne Division was established and organized along the lines of a US airborne division of the time. Thus, three brigades, each attached to one of the three German corps commands are: 25 Brigade at Schwarswald, 26 Brigade at Saarlouis, and 27 Brigade at Lippstadt. Each brigade is comprised of four battalions, three regular and one reserve. Within each battalion are a staff and supply company, two airborne infantry companies and two airborne anti-tank companies. Each brigade also has five independent companies: HQ, medical, supply, mortar, and engineer. A total of 2,808 men make up a Fallschirmjäger brigade. Although as this is written re-unification of Germany and possible pullout from NATO seems possible, the 1st Airborne Division currently still provides the primary German contingent for NATO's Allied Mobile Force (AMF). The 1st Airborne Division receives extensive air mobile as well as airborne training, and in response to the likelihood of having to face massive Soviet tank thrusts, the Fallschirmjägers receive intensive anti-tank training.

Airborne training for members of the division and other para-qualified German personnel is carried out at the Airborne School at Altenstadt. Advanced training is carried out at the Airborne Training Centre at Schongau for career airborne troops. Advanced airborne tactics. Halo training, and Ranger (Einzelkampfer) training are given at Schongau.

Einzelkampfer (roughly equivalent to US Rangers) training last four weeks and ten courses per year are run. All platoon leaders in the infantry, airborne, mountain and LRRP units must pass this course. Hence leadership as well as unarmed combat, obstacle crossing, mobility and survival are stressed.

Another extremely élite unit within the West German Army is the 1st Mountain Division, also established in 1956. Normal deployment for the division is: division HQ at Garmisch–Partenkirchen, 22nd Armoured Infantry Brigade at Murnau, 23rd Mountain Rifle Brigade at Bad Reichenhall, 24th Armoured Brigade at Landshut, and 56th Home Defence Brigade at Neuburg. The armoured/mechanized units are deployed in the lower Alps and the mountain infantry units in the high Alps. The mountain brigade has four mountain infantry battalions and one mountain artillery battalion, all trained for ski/high mountain operations. Other divisional troops include: a mountain artillery regiment, mountain communications battalion, mountain armoured recon battalion, mountain tank battalion, two separate mountain battalions, a security protection battalion, mountain aid defence battalion, mountain engineer regiment, mountain aviation squadron, mountain maintenance/repair battalion, mountain supply/support battalion, and a mountain medical services battalion. In all the 1st Mountain Division fields about 20,000 men. Virtually

PLATE 53: WEST GERMANY

1 Metal airborne beret badge minus national flag (obsolete)
2 Cloth airborne beret badge
3 Metal Fernspah beret badge
4 Cloth Fernspah beret badge
5 Mountain Guide qualification badge; made in bullion on grey, silk on grey, and silk on fatigue
6 Einzelkampfer badge; in cloth silver on fatigue for the Army and Luftwaffe, gold on fatigue for the Navy, and subdued for US personnel; in bullion, silver on grey for the Army; silver on blue grey for the Luftwaffe, and gold on blue or gold on white for the Navy
7, 8, 9 1st Airborne Division; borders indicate brigades
10, 11 New International LRRP School patches
12 Patch 3rd Company, 252 Airborne B, 25th Airborne Bde

13 Patch 2nd Company, 252 Airborne Bn, 25th Airborne Bde
14 Patch 3rd Company, 252 Airborne Bn, 25th Airborne Bde
15 Patch Airborne anti-tank company, 250th Airborne Bn, 25th Airborne Bde
16 Patch for Airborne Training Company 260
17 Patch 1st Company, 261st Airborne Bn, 26th Airborne Bde
18 Patch 3rd Company, 261st Airborne Bn, 26th Airborne Bde
19 Patch 4th Company, 261st Airborne Bn, 26th Airborne Bde
20 Patch 2nd Company, 262nd Airborne Bn, 26th Aviation Bde
21 Patch 271st Company, 27th Airborne Bde
22 Sport parachute club, 1st Airborne Division
23 Patch Airborne Signal Instructional, Bn 19

PLATE 53

1

2

3

4

5 HEERESBERGFÜHRER

6

7

8

9

10 S

11 L

12 3./Fallschirmjägerbataillon 252

13 2./Fsch Jg Btl 252

14 3./Fsch Jg Btl 252

15 LL PZ ABW KP 250

16 AUSB KP 260

17 261

18 FSCH JG BTL 261 3

19 FALLSCHIRMJÄGERBATAILLON 261 4 KOMPANIE

20 FSCH JG BTL 262 SUUM CUIQVE

21 FSC 271 JSERLOHN

22 FSC 2 LUFTLANDEDIVISION

23 LL Fm Lehr Bt 19 9

every member of the division receives basic ski and mountaineering training, while experienced alpinists are concentrated in the high mountain units. They receive highly specialized training at the high mountain school at Mittenwald.

Sometimes confused with the regular troops of the alpine units are the Mountain Guides who advise commanders on all aspects of mountain warfare and who provide the training cadre for the 1st Mountain Division. Once selected for Mountain Guide training, soldiers undergo a rigorous 32-week training regimen which produces some of the finest mountain-ski troops in the world.

Yet another highly élite unit within the West German Army is the Fernspah (what in the US Army would be called LRRPs). Each of the corps in the Bundswehr has its own Fernspah company to gather close-range Intelligence on enemy units identification, weapons and equipment, HQ sites, airfields, supply dumps, etc. These companies are numbered 100 for 1st Corps, 200 for 2nd Corps, and 300 for 3rd Corps. Primarily recruited from the airborne and mountain divisions, the Fernspah must still undergo specialized training in communications, land navigation, map reading, close combat, survival, escape and evasion, camouflage, infiltration and exfiltration, photography, Intelligence-gathering, and other such skills. Training takes place at the International Long Range Patrol School at Weingarten where No. 1 Wing conducts the famed international course for allied personnel, while No. 2 Wing trains West German Fernspah. Operationally, the Fernspahtrupp consisting of four men is the basic element.

Within the West German Navy are that country's underwater élite – the Kampfschwimmers. The combat swimmer company has such missions as reconnaissance of harbours, Intelligence-gathering, underwater sabotage, beach clearance, and raids from the sea or rivers. Combat swimmers are trained for insertion via parachute, small boat, or SCUBA.

Two distinctive berets are worn within the West German Army – maroon by the airborne troops and Fernspaher and green by the Einzelkampfers.

PLATE 54: WEST GERMANY

24 Patch 2nd Company, 261st Airborne Bn, 26th Airborne Bde
25 Unidentified
26 International LRRP School patch
27 Fernspah Parachutist Sport patch
28 LRRP Company 100 sport patch
29 LRRP Training Centre
30 LRRP Company 100
31 LRRP Company 200
32 LRRP Company 300
33 Combat Swimmer pocket patch
34 Another combat swimmer patch
35 HQ 25th Airborne Bde, pocket crest; note that to save space the following pocket crests would be on a similar hanger
36 Airborne Bn 251, 25th Airborne Bde pocket crest
37 Airborne Bn 252, 25th Airborne Bde pocket crest
38 Airborne Bn 253, 25th Airborne Bde pocket crest
39 Airborne Eng Company 250 (Type II), pocket crest
40 Avn Eng Company 250 (Type I), pocket crest
41 Airborne Mortar Company 250, pocket crest
42 Airborne Medical Company 250, pocket crest
43 Airborne Supply Company 250, pocket crest
44 Airborne Brigade 26, pocket crest
45 Airborne Bn 261, 26th Airborne Bde, pocket crest

▶ *These Germans have G3 rifles and a Lanze anti-tank weapon, making them a potent striking force. (Courtesy of Ian V. Hogg)*

PLATE 54

24

25

26

27

28

29

30

31

32

33

34

35

36

37

38

39

40

41

42

43

44

45

PLATE 55: WEST GERMANY

46 Airborne Bn 263, 26th Airborne Bde, pocket crest
47 Airborne Engineer Company 260, 26th Airborne Bde, pocket crest
48 Airborne Mortar Company 260, 26th Airborne Bde, pocket crest
49 Airborne Medical Company 260, 26th Airborne Bde, pocket crest
50 Airborne Supply Company 260, 26th Airborne Bde, pocket crest
51 Airborne Bn 262, 26th Airborne Bde, pocket crest; also worn by Airborne Signal Company 9
52 Airborne Anti-Tank Company 260, 26th Airborne Bde, pocket crest
53 27th Airborne Brigade, pocket crest
54 Airborne Bn 271, 27th Airborne Bde
55 Airborne Bn 272, 27th Airborne Bde
56 Airborne Bn 273, 27th Airborne Bde

57 Airborne Battalion 274, 27th Airborne Brigade
58 Airborne Engineer Company 270
59 Airborne Medical Company 270
60 Airborne Supply Company 270
61 Airborne Company 909, the instructional and test company at the Airborne School, pocket crest
62 Airborne School, pocket crest
63 International LRRP School
64 LRRP Company 100
65 LRRP Company 300
66 Mountain Artillery Company 81 (this unit is no longer airborne but is included since it retains the parachute on its crest)
67 12th Engineer Battalion (no longer airborne but retains parachute on crest)
68 Signal Training Company 3/11 (not airborne but included because of parachute on crest)

◄ *A good illustration of the extremes of terrain and temperature in which all special forces must be able to operate. These are German special mountain troops on a training exercise. (Courtesy of Ian V. Hogg)*

PLATE 55

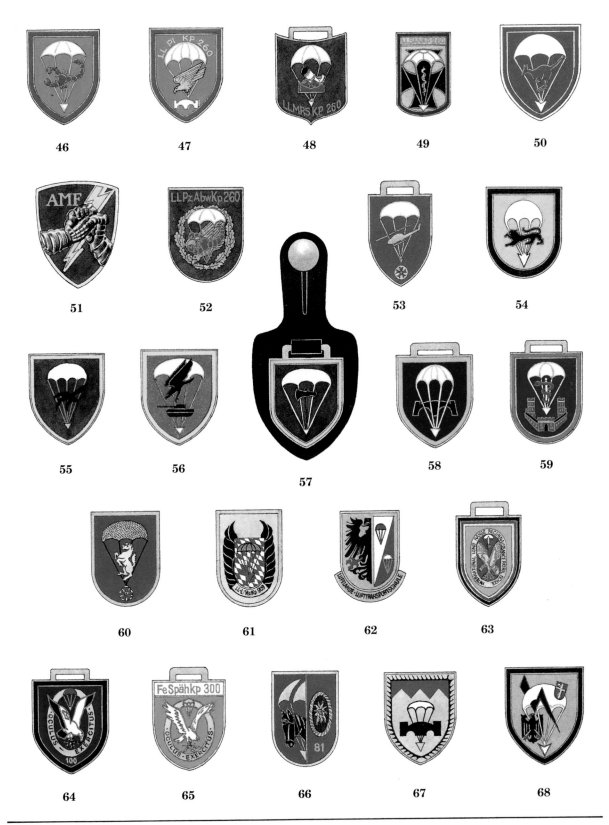

46

47

48

49

50

51

52

53

54

55

56

57

58

59

60

61

62

63

64

65

66

67

68

ITALY

Italy was a pioneer in the development of both airborne and scuba troops prior to and during the Second World War. This heritage has helped maintain Italian airborne and special operations units at a high standard. Italy's first post-war Army airborne unit was a parachute battalion formed in 1948. Throughout the 1950s other parachute units were formed including a parachute platoon within the Alpine Brigade, a Carabinieri Parachute Battalion, a Parachute Saboteur Battalion and a Parachute Artillery Battery. Drawing on these and other units, the 1st Parachute Regiment was formed in 1962, then expanded to brigade status the next year, though it did not receive its current designation as the Folgore Brigade until 1967. Within the Folgore Brigade are the following units: 1st Carabinieri Parachute Battalion 'Tuscania', 2nd Prachute Battalion 'Tarquinia', 3rd Parachute Battalion 'Poggio Rusco', 5th Parachute Battalion 'El Alamein', 9th Para Saboteur Battalion 'Col. Moschin', 185th Parachute Artillery Group 'Viterbo', 4th Alpine Parachute Company, and the Parachute School at Pisa. Other airborne-qualified units within the Army include parachute platoons assigned to each of the five alpine brigades, themselves élite mountaineering and ski units. The Saboteur Battalion normally operates in the Long Range Recon Patrol or raiding mission. The Carabinieri are the militarized national police, and in addition to providing military police support for the Folgore Brigade the airborne members of the Carabinieri can be used for other specialized missions. Members of GIS, the Carabinieri anti-terrorist unit,

are often drawn from the parachute battalion. As previously mentioned, the Alpini are another highly trained group within the Army. Each of the five Alpine brigades: Taurinese, Orobica, Tridentina, Cadore, and Julia, consists of an Alpine infantry regiment of 3–4 battalions, an Alpine engineer company, an aviation unit, a parachute platoon, an armoured infantry company with APCs, and an Alpine artillery regiment.

Often considered the most élite troops within the Italian armed forces are their 'incursori', the parachute frogmen. Known as COMSUBIN (Commando Raggruppamento Subacqui ed Incursori), the 200 men of the Incursori are headquartered just outside La Spezia. In addition to its normal combat swimmer tasks, CONSUBIN also handles Italian anti-terrorist duties for ship hijackings or other operations involving their special skills. Many members of CONSUBIN are drawn from the Italian Marines, the San Marco Battalion. This 1,000-man battalion is divided into an operations group of four companies, a logistics group, and a training group. Primarily specialists in amphibious operations, a large number of San Marco Marines are also parachute-trained.

One final unit that is airborne-trained is the Target Acquisitions Group for the 3rd Missile Brigade. This group trains extensively with American contingents to NATO and wears American as well as Italian parachute wings.

The members of the Folgore Brigade wear the traditional airborne maroon beret; the members of the San Marco Marines wear a black beret.

PLATE 56: ITALIAN AIRBORNE

1 Beret badge worn by airborne personnel not assigned to a unit with a numbered beret badge
2 Variant beret badge for members of the Folgore Brigade not assigned to a numbered unit
3 Beret badge for members of the Folgore Brigade assigned to a numbered unit; in this case the 9th Incursori Battalion
4 Alpini cap badge worn on the Alpini hat, but the small parachute denotes those Alpini who are on parachute status
5 Another, subdued, version of the Alpini hat badge
6 Other ranks' para beret badge worn until about 1963
7 Variant of the officers' para beret badge worn until about 1963
8 Officers' para beret badge worn until about 1963
9 Other ranks' subdued plastic para beret badge similar to

10 Beret badge worn by personnel assigned to the Italian Parachute School
11 Officers' subdued para beret badge similar to 8
12 Beret badge worn by the airborne target acquisition unit, 26th Gruppo Squadroni ALE
13 Distinctive insignia worn by airborne engineers from 1963 to 1975
14 Although sometimes identified as a variant of 13, this badge is most likely for an Air Force parachute unit known as 'Azzuro' from the 1940s
15 Collar badge worn by all members of the Folgore Brigade not assigned to a specialist unit
16 Collar badge worn by airborne artillery
17 Collar badge worn by airborne engineers
18 Collar badge worn by airborne signals
19 Collar badge worn by airborne medical
20 Collar badge worn by airborne equipment supply
21 Collar badge worn by airborne food supply
22 Collar badge worn by airborne administrative

PLATE 56

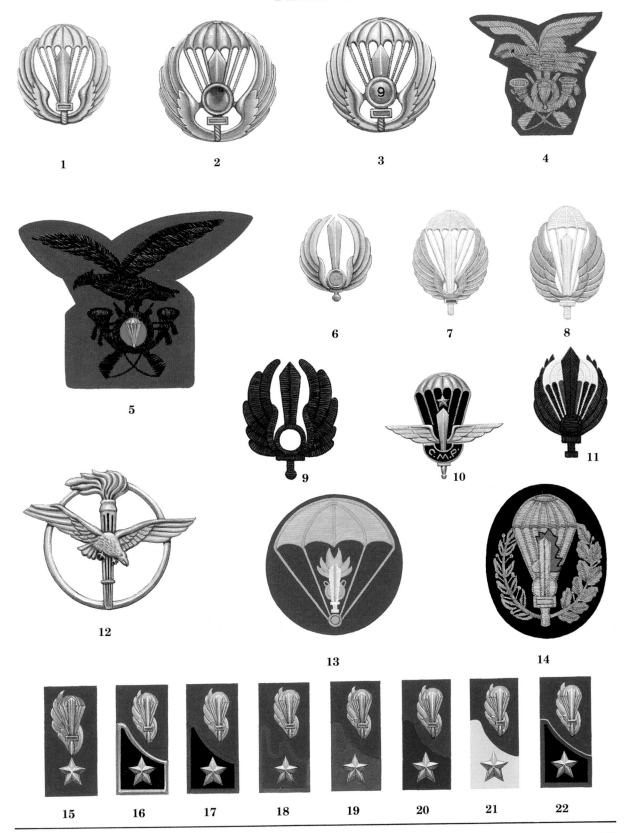

1

2

3

4

5

6

7

8

9

10

11

12

13

14

15 16 17 18 19 20 21 22

PLATE 57: ITALIAN AIRBORNE

23 Metal collar insignia worn by all ranks from 1946 to 1963

24 Collar insignia of the 1st Carabinieri Battalion 'Tuscania'

25 Bullion para collar insignia

26 Old-style Folgore Brigade bullion collar insignia

27 Other ranks' airborne collar insignia 1946–1963

28 Collar badge worn by non-parachute-qualified personnel of the Folgore Brigade (note lack of parachute on insignia)

29 Silk bevo parachutists' collar insignia

30 Air Force parachutists' collar insignia

31 Bullion version of No. 30

32 Obsolete distinctive insignia (DI) for the 1st Parachute Regiment

33 First-type DI for 1st Carabinieri Parachute Battalion 'Tuscania'

34 Second-type DI for 1st Carabinieri Parachute Battalion 'Tuscania'

35 First-type DI for 2nd Parachute Battalion 'Tarquinia'

36 Second-type DI for 2nd Parachute Battalion 'Tarquinia'

37 Obsolete 2nd Parachute Battalion DI

38 3rd Parachute Battalion 'Poggio Rusco' DI

39 First-type DI for 5th Parachute Battalion 'El Alamein'

40 Second-type DI for 5th Parachute Battalion 'El Alamein'

41 DI for 9th Parachute Battalion 'Col. Moschin'; INC stands for 'Incursori' designating this as a special assault/long-range patrol battalion. The yellow backing indicates six years of service, and the DI is mounted on a pocket hanger when wearing it on the uniform. Nos. 366–369 are also on their hangers. For winter the hangers are dark brown or black and for summer tan

42 The same as No. 41 but without the years of service backing

43 Similar to the badge in 40 and 41, but marked SAB for 'Sabatatore'; the red backing indicates ten years of service with the battalion. Blue would indicate eight years of service

44 DI for Parachute Signals Company, Folgore Brigade

45 DI for Parachute Maintenance Company, Folgore Brigade; 'Ripiegatore' means 'rigger'

▲An Italian airborne colonel wears parachute wings, airborne collar insignia and beret badge. (Adrian Bohlen)

PLATE 57

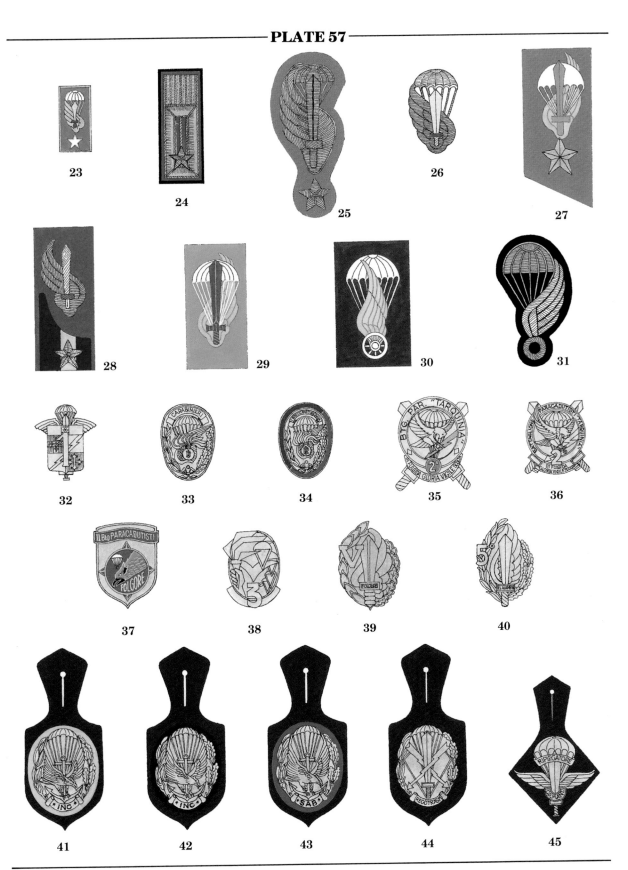

23

24

25

26

27

28

29

30

31

32

33

34

35

36

37

38

39

40

41

42

43

44

45

PLATE 58: ITALIAN AIRBORNE AND INCURSORI

46 DI for Parachute Platoon, Alpini Brigade 'Tridentina'
47 DI for Parachute Platoon. Alpini Brigade 'Cadore'
48 DI for Parachute Platoon, Alpini Brigade 'Orobica'
49 DI for Parachute Platoon, Alpini Brigade 'Taurinense'
50 DI for Parachute Company, Alpini IV C.d'A
51 DI for Parachute Aerial Resupply Company, Folgore Brigade
52 DI for HQ, Folgore Brigade
53 DI for 185th Parachute Field Artillery Group 'Viterbo', Folgore Brigade
54 DI for Parachute Logistics Battalion, Folgore Brigade
55 DI for Parachute Anti-Tank Company, Folgore Brigade
56 DI for Parachute Engineer Company, Folgore Brigade
57 DI for Parachute Command and Service Company, Folgore Brigade (second type)
58 DI for Airborne Medical Company, Folgore Brigade
59 DI for Parachute Maintenance Company, Carabinieri Parachute Battalion
60 DI for Parachute Reconnaissance Company, Folgore Brigade
61 DI for Parachute Long Range Patrol Battalion 'Sabatatore' (first type)
62 DI for Battalion 'Sabatatore' (second type)
63 DI for Military Parachute School cadre
64 Parachute Instructor's qualification badge
65 Second World War RSI Airborne insignia, included because it is often mistaken for current distinctive insignia
1 Incursori qualification badge for petty officers 1st and 2nd class to be worn on the shoulder boards on the summer uniform and on the sleeve in winter uniform
2 Variation on Incursori qualification for petty officers 1st and 2nd class
3 Incursori qualification badge for chief petty officers and officers to be worn over the ribbons on the left pocket
4 Variation of the Incursori qualification badge for CPOs and officers
5 Army Commando qualification badge
6 Variation of No. 5

▲Italian airborne NCO of the Parachute Signals Company (note the crest on the left pocket). (Adrian Bohlen)

PLATE 58

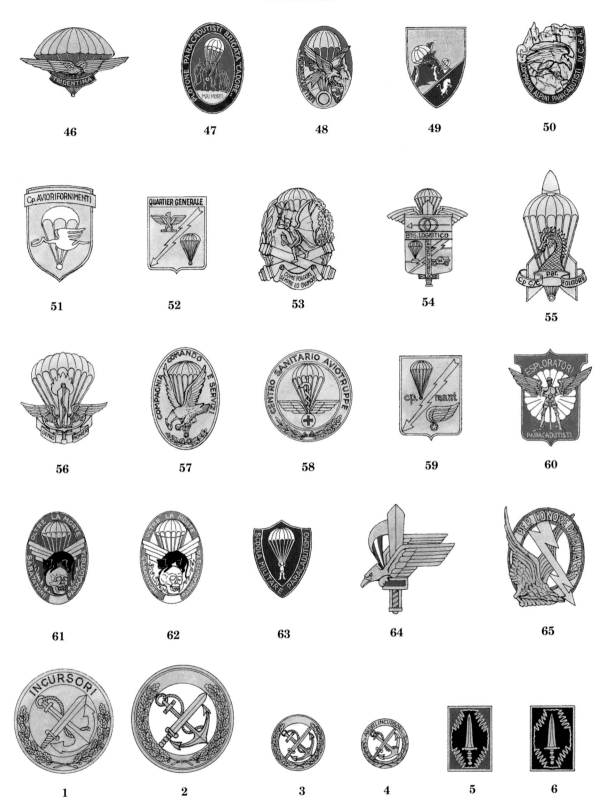

46

47

48

49

50

51

52

53

54

55

56

57

58

59

60

61

62

63

64

65

1

2

3

4

5

6

PLATE 59: ITALIAN MARINES AND AIRBORNE

1 COMSUBIN Frogman/Para-Frogman other ranks' qualification badge
2 CONSUBIN officer qualification badge
3 San Marco Marine DI
4 San Marco Marine collar insignia
5 San Marco Marine beret badge
1 Original Folgore Parachute Brigade sleeve insignia, bullion: note, such insignia are known as 'scudetti' (shields)
2 Original Folgore Parachute Brigade sleeve insignia, cloth or plastic
3 Current Folgore Brigade sleeve insignia, bullion
4 Current Folgore Brigade sleeve insignia, cloth or plastic
5 Early post-Second World War Folgore Combat Group sleeve insignia, bullion
6 Early post-Second World War Folgore Combat Group sleeve insignia, cloth or plastic
7 Bullion insignia for the support company at the Military Parachute school
8 Rubberized plastic version of No. 7
9 Military Parachute School sleeve insignia, bullion
10 Military Parachute School sleeve insignia, cloth or plastic
11 Parachute Instructor's patch: note that the word at the top of the patch is not 'SNIPER' but 'SMIPAR' standing for School, Military, Parachute
12 Folgore Brigade sport parachute patch
13 5th Company, 2nd Parachute Battalion sport patch
14 Silk patch for the Parachute Recondo Company

◀ *These are members of the Italian Special Forces, the Nucleo Operativio Centrale di Sicurezza (NOCS), whose standard equipment includes the Beretta Model 12 submachine-gun and the Beretta Model 92 SB pistol, both visible here.*

PLATE 59

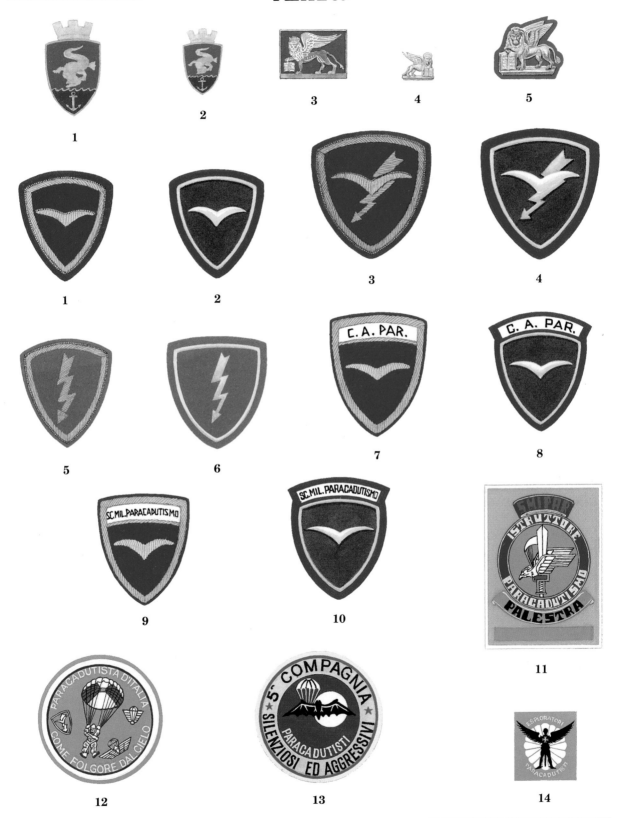

1

2

3

4

5

1

2

3

4

5

6

7

C. A. PAR.

8

9

SC. MIL. PARACADUTISMO

10

11

12

13

14

PLATE 60: ITALIAN CLOTH PARACHUTE INSIGNIA AND TURKISH INSIGNIA

15 Silk insignia for the 2nd Battalion of the Folgore Brigade. Colours designate companies: green, 4th Company
16 Blue, 5th Company
17 Maroon, 6th Company
18 Black, alternate pattern of 4th Company
19 Red, alternate pattern of 6th Company
20 Yellow, heavy weapons company
21 Patch for Target Acquisitions Unit of the Folgore Brigade

22 Pocket patch for the 14th Company of the 5th Parachute Battalion
23 Pocket patch for the HQ Company of the 5th Parachute Battalion
24 Pocket patch for the 15th Parachute Company
25 Shoulder Patch of the Commando and Service Company of the Parachute School
26 Unidentified.
27 Shoulder patch for the Aerial Supply Company of the Parachute School

TURKEY

Turkish troops are legendary for their toughness which has given that country's special operations forces a good manpower pool to select from. Currently Turkey has one airborne brigade, one Commando brigade, and one marine brigade. Due to mountainous terrain in much of Turkey the Commando Brigade has received extensive training in mountain warfare. Additionally, the Turkish Air Force has trained parachute troops as have the Jandara, the national police. The counter-terrorist unit of the latter, particularly, have received parachute, mountain, and Commando training.

Because of the closeness of the Soviet Union to their borders, the Turks have also emphasized the training of their special operations troops to form local guerrilla groups within Turkey. During the fighting in Cyprus in 1974, the Turkish Airborne Brigade was committed against Greek Cypriots in support of Turks on the island. Some jumped in and some were inserted via helicopter.

PLATE 60 CONTINUED: TURKEY

1 Parachute rigger badge
2 Unidentified Turkish parachute unit (*c.* 1960s)
3 Command shoulder sleeve insignia
4 Para Commando shoulder sleeve insignia
5 Commando qualification badge
6 Commando and Mountain Warfare School badge
7 Gendarmerie Commando School badge
8 12th Aerial Delivery Company
9 Commando qualification badge
10 Cloth version of No. 6
11 Variation of No. 10
12 Gendarmerie breast qualification badge
13 Free-fall parachute patch

▶Turkish paratrooper wearing the 'air landing' insignia on his left breast. (Adrian Bohlen)

PLATE 60

15

16

17

18

19

20

21

22

23

24

25

26

27

1

2

3

4

5

6

7

8

9

10

11

12

13

SPAIN

Although they were air-lifted rather than dropped by parachute, Spanish Foreign Legion troops under Franco, brought from North Africa by aircraft, played a critical role in the Spanish Civil War. Soviet-trained Commando units such as that immortalized by Hemingway in *For Whom The Bell Tolls* operated on the other side during the Spanish Civil War. Some of these Soviet-trained troops as well as some Nationalists trained by the Germans received parachute training during 1938. Post-Second World War a few members of the Spanish Air Force received parachute training in Argentina and formed the nucleus for a Spanish parachute school at Alcantarilla Air Base. Within the Air Force a battalion of parachute troops was trained and operational by 1949.

It was not until five years later that the Army trained its own parachutists, the 1st Parachute Battalion, in February 1954. In 1956 the 2nd Battalion was formed, and in 1960 the 3rd Battalion was formed. The Army now formed its own parachute depot and training school at Murcia in 1961. 1958 had seen the first combat jump by Spanish paratroopers in Morocco in conjunction with French paras. In February, 1965, a Parachute Brigade was formed incorporating the three battalions as well as an artillery battalion, engineer battalion, mixed support battalion, and training bat-

talion; all parachute-qualified. Within the brigade are specialist HALO companies to act as pathfinders or for other special missions. The members of the Parachute Brigade wear a distinctive black beret.

There are also the COE (Companias de Operaciones Especciales) or special forces companies. Highly trained in small unit operations, survival, guerrilla, and counter-guerrilla operations, the COEs would have the mission of forming guerrilla movements within Spain should the country be invbaded. They wear green berets.

The Spanish Air Force maintains three parachute companies who wear distinctive blue berets. Spanish combat swimmers receive parachute training as well.

The Spanish Foreign Legion is not as well known as the French Foreign Legion, but it is considered an élite light infantry formation within the Spanish Armed Forces. Though formerly 10–15 per cent of its strength was foreign, all recruits are now Spanish citizens. The Legion also maintains its own Special Operations Unit based at Ronda which adds scuba, parachuting, hand-to-hand combat, guerrilla and counter-guerrilla warfare to the Legion's excellent small unit training. Members of the Spanish Foreign Legion also wear green berets.

PLATE 61: SPAIN

1 Airborne beret badge
2 Unidentified
3 Special operations beret badge
4 Variant of No. 3
5 Cloth special operations beret badge
6 Shoulder sleeve insignia of the Airborne Brigade
7 Subdued version of No. 6
8 Airborne artillery SSI
9 1st Airborne Battalion SSI
10 Airborne command and control SSI
11 3rd Airborne Battalion SSI
12 Engineers
13 2nd Airborne Battalion
14 Airborne logistics group SSI

15 Unidentified
16 Special operations companies SSI
17 Special operations qualification badge
18 Variant of special operations qualification badge
19 Variant of special operations qualification badge
20 Officers' airborne collar insignia
21 Other ranks' airborne collar insignia
22 Three years' airborne service badge in metal
23 Three years' airborne service badge in cloth
24 Variant of metal three years' airborne service
25 Four years' airborne service badge; note, the eagle clutching the parachute is the basic award while each stripe indicates an additional year of airborne service
26 Five years' airborne service
27 Six years' airborne service

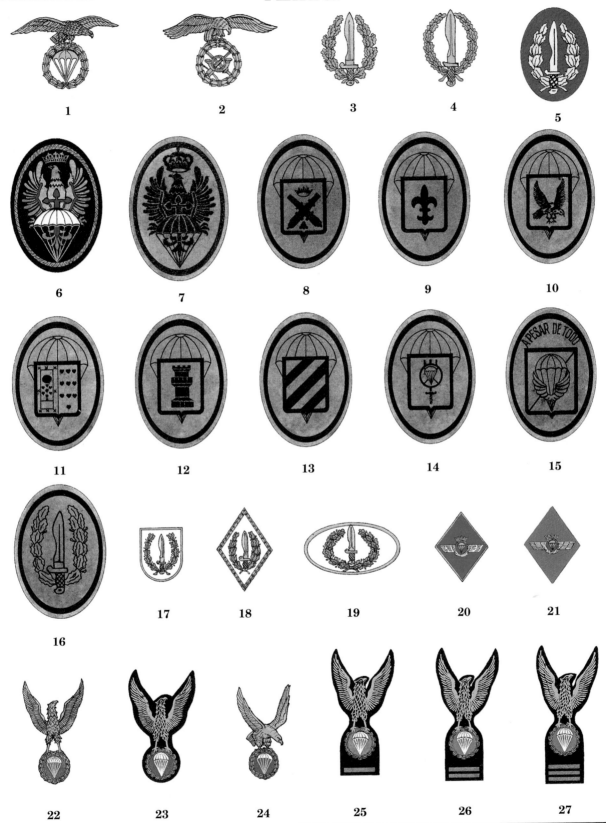

PLATE 61

1

2

3

4

5

6

7

8

9

10

11

12

13

14

15

16

17

18

19

20

21

22

23

24

25

26

27

PLATE 62: SPAIN

28 Pocket crest worn on a fob for the HQ unit of the Parachute Brigade
29 Pocket crest for the Para Brigade training battalion; also worn by instructors
30 Para Brigade mixed support battalion pocket crest
31 Para Brigade engineer group pocket crest
32 Para Brigade artillery group pocket crest
33 Unidentified
34 Para Brigade pocket crest
35 1st Para Battalion pocket crest
36 2nd Para Battalion pocket crest
37 3rd Para Battalion pocket crest

38 Special Operations shoulder arc
39 Naval special operations subdued patch
40 62nd Special Operations Company subdued patch
41 92nd Special Operations Company subdued patch
42 101st Special Operations Company subdued patch
43 103rd Special Operations Company coloured patch
44 Sleeve insignia of the Unidad Especial de Intervencion, the hostage rescue unit of the Guardia Civil
45 Special Operations Company of the Spanish Foreign Legion patch
46 Pocket crest of the Grupo Especial de Operaciones, the hostage rescue unit of the Policia Nacional

PORTUGAL

Portugal has had airborne troops since 1955 as part of the Air Force. During the colonial wars in Africa, the parachute troops were organized into a parachute regiment and four separate battalions. The separate battalions were for service in the colonies – one in Guinea, one in Angola, and two in Mozambique. Portuguese parachutists go through jump training at Tencos which is also the home of the Parachute Regiment. This training takes 31 weeks, the first fourteen basic and advanced infantry training, then four weeks of actual jump training which includes eight jumps, then finally thirteen weeks of advanced infantry and tactical training. Since 1961 female para-nurses have attended a 3-month course at the same school. During the counter-insurgency wars in Africa it was standard for recent graduates of the airborne school to serve two years overseas with one of the combat units then return to the parent regiment.

Portugal has also had many separate Commando units, once again primarily for service in the colonies. A Special Operations School at Lamego taught a 10-week course particularly for officers and NCOs being sent to Africa. Overseas Commando schools were also maintained for training indigenous black Commando troops in the colonies. These local schools were also used to give Portuguese Commandos an additional four weeks of acclimatization training.

Another unit of special interest designed for service in the colonies was the CACADORES, élite light infantry units roughly equivalent to the US Rangers. Their specialties were raids, ambushes, and counter-insurgency.

Finally, within the Portuguese Marines there are special Commando-trained detachments as well as a small number of combat swimmers.

Airborne troops wear the green beret; Commandos wear the red beret.

PLATE 62: CONTINUED: PORTUGAL

1 Current pocket crest for the Airborne School
2 Pocket crest for CMI parachutists
3 1st Cie, Cacadores Para, 21st Battalion
4 Pocket crest of Operational Base No. 1, Lisbon
5 Corps de Policia parachutists
6 Unidentified
7 111 Cacadores parachutists
8 Airborne HQ
9 Commandos metal shoulder arc
10 Special operations metal shoulder arc
11 Commandos' breast pin

PLATE 62

28

29

30

31

32

33

34

35

36

37

38

39

40

41

42

43

44

45

46

1

2

3

4

5

6

7

8

9

10

11

PLATE 63: SWITZERLAND

Switzerland maintains only one small but élite airborne formation, the 17th Parachute Grenadier Company of the Swiss Air Force. It was first decided that Switzerland needed an airborne raiding and recon element in 1968, but the first school for military parachutists was not run until 1970. Over the next four years a school was run each year to bring the unit to strength, then from 1974 until 1982 schools were run every two years. Beginning in 1982 schools have again been run every year. In 1980 the para grenadiers were assigned their current long-range patrol/sabotage mission. An important note, by the way, is that the 17th Parachute Grenadier Company is the only Swiss unit with the mission of operating across Swiss borders in time of conflict.

Those interested in joining the 17th Company go through a rigorous selection process. At the age of 17, interviews and aptitude tests are given; those selected then undergo a 2-week basic parachute course including ten static line jumps. Most operational jumps in Switzerland would be free-fall, however, so at the age of 18 candidates undergo additional free-fall training during which they make forty jumps. Successful completion of this phase qualifies them for five months of additional training including a 5-week advanced military tactical parachute course during which they make at least 80 more jumps including day and night, full equipment, and low-level jumps. So intensive is the

training that out of 300 or more candidates only 12–15 will normally make it all the way through. Additional Commando/LRRP training is ongoing.

Normally the only distinctive insignia worn on the combat uniform by the Grenadier Paras is a shoulder slide bearing the numeral '17', but their fibre jump helmet also helps identify them. Additional insignia may be worn on dress uniforms or on sports clothing.

1 Para Grenadier collar insignia
2 Opposite collar of 613
3 17th Para Grenadier Company shoulder slide
4 Infantry grenadier (non-airborne but considered élite within the Swiss Army) collar insignia
5 Infantry grenadier sleeve insignia
6 Assault engineers (élite assault troops) sleeve insignia
7 17th Para Grenadier Company patch
8 Combat swimmer qualification
9 Combat swimmer/small boat collar insignia
10 1971 para selection course sport patch (awarded along with their wings to those successfully completing the course)
11 1972 para selection course sport patch
12 1973 selection course patch
13 1974 selection course patch
14 1976 selection course patch
15 1978 selection course patch
16 1980 selection course patch
17 1982 selection course patch
18 Grenadier para patch

◄A member of Switzerland's 17th Grenadier Parachute Company shows the shoulder slide worn on the combat dress. (Adrian Bohlen)

PLATE 63

1

2

3

4

5

6

7

8

9

10

11

12

13

14

15

16

17

18

PLATE 64: CZECHOSLOVAKIA

Prior to the 1968 Soviet invasion, the Czechs deployed an airborne brigade – the *Vysadkova Brigada*, but during the post-invasion period, airborne strength was cut back to regimental strength, stationed near Prosnice. The regiment appears to have four battalions: one active parachute, one active special operations, one reserve, and one training.

Czech parachute training includes a basic five jumps during a one-month airborne school for the award of the 3rd Class parachute brevet. Ten jumps, including day and night jumps and equipment jumps, are required for the 2nd Class brevet. The 1st Class brevet is awarded after 25 jumps. To receive the Instructor's brevet, it is necessary to make 50 jumps including tree jumps, water jumps, and free-fall jumps, the latter including target accuracy of the descent. To receive the highest award of Master Parachutist requires 250 jumps which include at least twenty water jumps, five tree jumps, twenty night jumps, five jumps wearing gas mask, five jumps carrying a radio, and five jumps carrying a crew-served weapon. Only officers and NCOs are eligible for award of the Instructor and Master brevets. Members of the Czech Air Force also receive training which also includes maintenance of the chutes carried in the seat pack on jets and, for the more advanced ratings, ejection-seat jumps.

Czech airborne troops wear an interesting maroon beret for dress uniform, but the same beret can be turned inside out whereupon it becomes a camo beret for field wear.

1 Airborne sleeve insignia 1948–59 in silk
2 Same as No. 1 in cloth
3 Diamond-shaped sleeve insignia worn by airborne troops from 1962 to the present. This one is for the Diversion Group
4 Tactical Recon troops
5 Special Anti-tank Group
6 Special Strategic Recon
7 Airborne Brigade
8 Airborne School

PLATE 64 CONTINUED: SOVIET UNION

The Soviet Union was the first country to experiment with airborne troops, and this interest has continued to the present as the Soviet Union fields seven airborne divisions, though as this is written it appears some will be disbanded. Each airborne division has three airborne regiments as well as support arms. The divisions are rather small (about 6,500 troops) and are heavily mechanized with 320 BMD armoured fighting vehicles. The airborne forces saw heavy combat in Afghanistan as élite light infantry and as air assault troops. Soviet paratroopers also took part in the invasion of Czechoslovakia and were poised for commitment in the Middle East during the 1973 Yom Kippur War.

Another élite within the Soviet armed forces is the Naval Infantry, the equivalent of the USMC or the Royal Marines. There are four naval infantry regiments, two assigned to the Black Sea Fleet, one to the Baltic Fleet, and one to the Northern Fleet. Each of these regiments is broken down into three amphibious motor rifle battalions with BTR-60 amphibious armoured troop carriers, and one naval tank battalion with PT-76 amphibious tanks and T-55 or T-72 tanks. Many members of the Naval Infantry are also airborne/air assault-qualified.

Soviet special forces are known as Spetsnaz and fall within the GRU (military intelligence). There are Army spetsnaz who would function in raiding missions of the SAS or US Ranger type, and naval Spetsnaz who would function much as the US SEALs or Marine RECONs or the British SBS. They are specifically targeted at NATO nuclear installations and with the assassination of high-ranking political and military personnel. There are also specialized personnel within the KGB known as Osnaz with similar missions.

Soviet élite forces wear berets as follows: airborne troops a light blue, naval infantry black. Spetsnaz often wear these same berets.

1 Airborne troops arm badge
2 Airborne troops shoulder board
3 Naval Infantry arm badge

PLATE 64

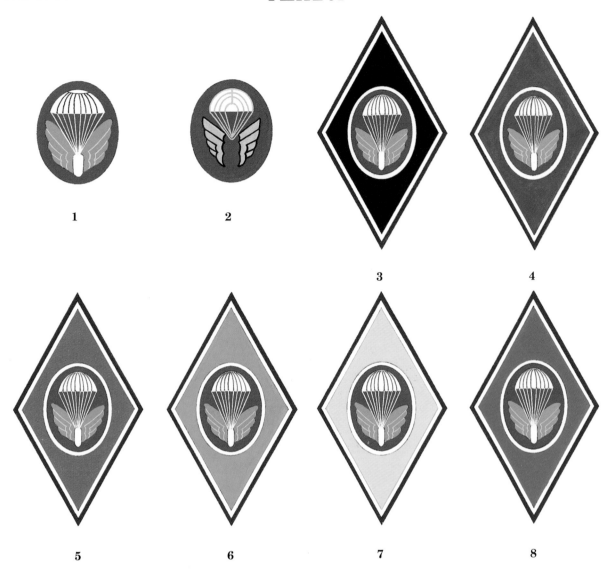

1

2

3

4

5

6

7

8

1

2

3

▲Soviet paratroopers wear the airborne beret, parachutists badge, airborne shoulder insignia and the distinctive striped T-shirt.

◀Soviet airlanding troops wearing camouflage and service caps move out from a Hind helicopter.

▲Spanish airborne NCO offers a good view of various parachute insignia including airborne collar insignia. (Adrian Bohlen)

▲Spanish paratrooper; note the beret badge and shoulder sleeve insignia. (Adrian Bohlen)

▲Brazilian wearing what appears to be the yellow bordered black backing to his parachute wings which indicates service in the Special Forces.

▲Brazilian Air Force NCO, probably with the parachute rescue unit. (Adrian Bohlen)

▲Danish Jäger sports not only Danish parachute brevet but US and French brevets as well. (Adrian Bohlen)

▲Turkish air force paratrooper; note qualification badges on the left breast including mountain/ski and Commando. (Adrian Bohlen)

◀Thai paratrooper wearing maroon beret and both parachute brevet and Ranger qualification badge. (Adrian Bohlen)